Investing Smart from the Start

The Beginner's Guide to Investing

DICK GOLDBERG

Longman Financial Services Publishing
a division of Longman Financial Services Institute, Inc.

While a great deal of care has been taken to provide accurate and current information, the ideas, suggestions, general principles and conclusions presented in this book are subject to local, state and federal laws and regulations, court cases and any revisions of same. The reader is thus urged to consult legal counsel regarding any points of law—this publication should not be used as a substitute for competent legal advice.

Executive Editor: Kathleen A. Welton
Project Editor: Roseann P. Costello
Copy Editor: Maija Balagot
Cover Design: Bob Cooley

© 1988 by Longman Group USA Inc.

Published by Longman Financial Services Publishing
a division of Longman Financial Services Institute, Inc.

Printed in the United States of America.

89 90 10 9 8 7 6 5 4 3 2

Library of Congress Cataloging-in-Publication Data
Goldberg, Dick, 1943-
    Investing smart from the start.
    Includes index.
    1. Investments—Handbooks, manuals, etc.
I. Title.
HG4527.G64 1988   332.6'78   88-533
ISBN 0-88462-737-3

Dedication

This book is dedicated to those who think for themselves—to the individualists: to Milton Friedman, who espoused market economics in the 1960s and early 1970s and was ridiculed by academia nationwide; to Edward R. Murrow, who stood alone in media to criticize the Communist witchhunts of the 1950s; to Betty Friedan, who laid the foundation of modern feminism while Avon Cosmetics stock was as hot as a comet, and to all those business people and investors who trust their gut—who look around themselves and say, "You're all nuts," and place their bets against the standard wisdom of the moment.

Author's Note

It's tough to title a book in ten words or less, but for a cover, that's all the room you've got. If I had all the space I needed, the title of this book would be:

The Book for the Person Who Wants To Learn All About Investments,
Who Doesn't Know Too Much About the Subject Now
or
Who Wants To Refresh What They Know,
Who Wants To Learn It Painlessly and Quickly,
Who Wants To Have a Good Time Doing It,
Who Wants To Know the Terms and Know the Players,
Who Wants To Be Able To Invest Wisely and Profitably
and
Who Wants To Never, Ever Get Taken

In other words, the book that, in a flight from New York to Los Angeles, can take you from investment illiteracy to investment wisdom.

Contents

Foreword

Although I consider myself a seasoned investor, I found many practical tips in Dick Goldberg's comprehensive investment guide. While this book was written, as its title suggests, for the beginning investor, it behooves many experienced investors to get back to basics every once and awhile. Professional golfers who find themselves at the top of the money-winning list season after season know this lesson well. During the year they frequently rush home to their teaching pros when they find their shots landing in the rough too often. Their games are quickly put back on course when their mentors detect and correct slight departures from the basic fundamentals of the golf swing. The same idea is applicable to experienced investors who find that they must return to the basics of their wealth-building strategies when their investments land in the rough once too often.

The novice investor will be, without a doubt, the greatest beneficiary of the wisdom presented in **Investing Smart from** the Start. Through the use of this guide, beginners can view investment opportunities as they spring up with a sharp eye for financial advantages and/or disadvantages. Through Dick Goldberg's experiences, they can save years of costly mistakes by avoiding certain pitfalls associated with specific investments. I wish I had come across a book such as **Investing Smart from the Start** early in my investment career so that I could have saved several years of wasted effort and could have begun a meaningful wealth-building program from the start.

While in school I was introduced to the magic of compound investment return. Mathematically, the compound investment growth model is expressed as follows:

$$\text{Wealth} = \text{Investment} \, (1 + \text{Annual Return})^{\text{Years}}$$

That is, terminal wealth equals initial investment multiplied by one plus the annual rate of return earned, raised to a power equal to the number of years of that investment program. It was many years later that I learned that the most important variable on the right-hand side of the equation was the number of years the investment program was in effect, not the amount invested or return earned. Thus, the young are blessed with the ability to build wealth through their long investment lifetimes ahead of them, provided that they avoid catastrophic investment errors. **Investing Smart from the Start** provides the keys that can be used by novice investors to recognize and steer clear of investment mistakes, thereby lengthening the time during which meaningful investment returns can be earned.

Over the last twenty-five years, common stock investors who were able to stay in the game earned an average annual compound rate of return of twelve percent. While this return may appear to be small by current yield standards, the long-term-oriented common stock investor who earned this average rate of return over the last twenty-five years would have seen his or her initial investment dollars grow by over sixteen times! Furthermore, because these average returns outstripped the rate of inflation of 9 percent annually, real wealth would have increased more than sevenfold. Investors who avoided large errors or took slightly higher than average investment risks and were able to earn a 15 percent rate of return rather than a 12 percent rate of return, would have seen their initial investments grow thirty-fold and their real wealth increase by more than 750 percent over the last quarter-century.

The moral of this investment tale should be clear. Start investing early, increase investment return by avoiding costly mistakes and enjoy the fruits of a successful investment lifetime. **Investing Smart from the Start** provides valuable assistance in increasing the odds of investment success. It should be read by all investors at least once and by the novice investor several times before he or she embarks on a lifetime investment program.

Gerald W. Perritt
Editor of *The Mutual Fund Letter* and *Investment Horizons*

Acknowledgment

I'd like to thank all those teachers—the ones at the Wharton School and at the University of Wisconsin and, perhaps even more so, the ones out there in the investment marketplace—all those who took a few minutes or a few hours to lend their advice and pass on some of the wisdom they gained from their experiences.

I'd also like to thank those people who were guests on radio and television programs I've done for more than the past eight years for providing an added perspective of reality in the business world.

Last but not least, I'd like to thank Katie Kazan for her most valuable and patient efforts at editing this book so that it is more readable and enjoyable, and Jean Nielsen for her cheerful and competent assistance in organizing research and typing the manuscript.

Introduction

Ultimately, you must trust yourself in making investment decisions. This is as it should be, because at the heart of those decisions is a commodity that is not guaranteed by professional credentials: common sense.

This book is intended to be the first book read before investing. You don't need "big bucks" to get started. It's for the person who has a considerable amount of money and must make decisions about its safekeeping and growth, or for the person who has very little money and wants to build wealth. As a matter of fact, as you'll learn in Chapter 1, sometimes there are advantages to being a very small investor.

Reading this book will make you investment-literate quickly and painlessly, and you'll even have some fun. In the four to six hours it will take you to read it, you'll have accomplished a lot. Investments will be demystified. Not only will you understand all the investment vehicles listed in the Contents, from common stocks to precious metals, you'll also be comfortable investigating any investments you didn't learn about in this book.

The typical way of investing in this country has been to place money into the hands of investment professionals. My experience, unfortunately, has been that these individuals, well dressed and confidence-inspiring as they may be, are wrong more often than they are right. As they sit at their desks, credentials prominently displayed, they look knowledgeable, sophisticated and intimidating. However, they frequently can't see the forest for the trees. In the middle of the daily ups and downs of the market, they have a difficult time taking the broad view, which is ultimately necessary for success.

Plus, I have even worse news. Most of these investment professionals are salespeople working on commission, whether they are stockbrokers, realtors or insurance salespeople. Their personal income depends on their making sales more than the wisdom of their choices. Therefore, in relying on them, you have two strikes against you: Their training or experience may be mostly sales-oriented, and their financial best interest may be at odds with your own. Ultimately, you must trust yourself in making investment decisions. This is as it should be, because at the heart of those decisions is a commodity that is not guaranteed by professional credentials: common sense.

No book can cover all available investments. There's a new one every day, with a new stripe, color, name or angle. However, if you know the right questions to ask, you can understand any investment vehicle and determine whether it's a good choice for you. Self-reliance in making investment decisions and planning your financial future is the goal of this book. I do not suggest that you never consult with professionals. Go ahead, get their advice and use their technical skills and ideas. In the end, however, you should be in control and make your own decisions. After you've read this book, I hope you'll be uncomfortable doing it any other way.

1

Money and What To Do
with It

*Remember, good money management is a matter of intelligent
—and* learned*—decision making and not some inherent
ability possessed only by a lucky few.*

If you ever save part of your paycheck, you are involved in the
business of money management. Whether you put your
money in a savings account, underneath your mattress, buy
stocks, bonds or a lottery ticket, etc., you're making a judgment about the best investment outlet for your funds.

If you know nothing about investments, you may try to
avoid the whole issue by putting your money in the bank.
You're not avoiding anything—you're making a clear-cut investment decision. You're saying, "This is the best alternative
for me, or at least the best alternative within my scope of
knowledge." You may also be implicitly saying that you're putting your money where there's no risk because you think you
lack the wisdom to make an intelligent investment. However,
there is always some risk, even with banks. Remember, good
money management is a matter of intelligent—and *learned*—
decision making and not some inherent ability possessed only
by a lucky few.

Investing is not an area only for the rich or well-to-do. It can and should reach equally the lives of those making $10,000 or $1,000,000 a year. Don't believe that just because you don't have the clout of the rich that you are automatically stuck with low rates of return on your money. I once noticed an over-the-counter stock called Barry Jewelers. The stock was selling at $1.50 per share. After analyzing the stock with methods you will learn later in this book, I decided the stock really was worth from $6 to $10 per share and would one day in the relatively near future sell in that range. So I ordered 10,000 shares at $1.50 per share. However, my stockbroker discovered that only 200 shares were available at that price. Since that meant I would be able to invest only $300, I decided to forget it—that amount was simply too small to have a significant impact on my financial position, and it would have taken too much of my time to watch it. Barry Jewelers was a small company and there was little activity in the trading of the stock. Just as I had anticipated, however, 18 months later the stock was selling at $12.50 per share. *The moral:* A small investor in a position to buy this stock could have made a return almost ten times greater than the initial money invested, whereas the well-heeled investor would be likely to pass up such a small deal.

This type of investment could be your opportunity. Often it is just these companies—overlooked by the wealthier investors—that offer exceptionally high rates of return.

There are places other than the stock market in which to invest your money. This book will explain your options so you'll know which investment vehicles are right for you and how to proceed once you've decided where to invest. Among the areas to be discussed are stocks, bonds, real estate, franchises, small businesses, commodities, options, coins, stamps and other collectibles, gold and silver, money market funds, life insurance, IRAs and Keoghs. Not all of these, of course, are going to be right for you. In fact, some, as you'll see, are not investments at all, but something altogether different.

There are many ways to use your money and to make your money work for you. Some of the better ones are so mundane that one may tend to overlook them; others are so exotic that they don't warrant discussion in a book dedicated to the small or inexperienced investor. Keep in mind that you will have the tools to analyze almost any investment and to determine if it's right for you.

My goal is to give you the foundation. The advice in this book, I firmly believe from personal experience, is the best route to follow whether you are a small *or* large investor. Find the direction best suited for you and pursue it, build on it. You cannot only take charge, but have success and fun doing it.

Cash

If I had to wager, I'd bet that in the next 50 years we won't see a run on the banks again, but ...

What is the most common investment for the "noninvestor?" It's "money in the bank," or in a savings and loan institution. Most people feel that this way they're safe: There's no risk involved. They also feel they're not making investments. On both points they're mistaken.

What are the risks in putting your money (investing it) in a checking account in a commercial bank? The first risk that comes to mind is, obviously, what if the bank goes broke? If the bank is not insured by the Federal Deposit Insurance Corporation (FDIC), you risk losing some or all of the money you put in the bank. (All federal banks are required to be insured by the FDIC. State-chartered banks are not required to carry FDIC insurance, but almost always do. Check it out.) It is not impossible for a bank to go broke; it happens all the time—just like fires happen all the time. It's not likely to happen, but any one bank can make a lot of bad loans, or have a dishonest president, or have assets dissolved by an earthquake or a flood or some such "act of God" in a land area in which it has a lot of outstanding loans. Most investors know enough to check and see that a bank is insured by FDIC before they deposit their money. They also know that if they deposit more than $100,000 in any one account, the FDIC won't insure the amount above $100,000. So be sure not to put more than $100,000 in one account. If you have to, go to several banks and open several accounts so that you have less than $100,000 in each account in each bank.

If the bank is insured by the FDIC is there still a risk? Well, yes and no. If your bank went broke and was covered by the FDIC, then there would be no risk; the FDIC would make sure that you would not lose any of the $100,000 in your account. The FDIC operates like any insurance company—on the law of odds and large numbers. A fire insurance company knows there will be one fire for every 5,000 or 10,000 homes they insure and the premiums from the other homes will pay for that fire. Similarly, the FDIC knows that in a year, there might be one bankruptcy for every 10,000 to 20,000 banks and that the premiums they collect from all the banks in their system will more than pay for the losses it suffers from those few banks that do go bankrupt. This means that as long as the economic system stays reasonably under control and the banking system does the same, the FDIC will protect you if it turns out that your money is deposited in a bank that's poorly managed. There is, however, the risk of a major national economic catastrophe, such as occurred in the 1930s. If there is a wave of distressed banks—if one bank's collapse brings about the collapse of another and another—and if at one time the entire national banking system collapses, the FDIC will not be able to meet all these claims. The FDIC is presently insuring over $1¼ trillion ($1,250 billion) in deposits but has a reserve of $18 billion, plus $3 billion in borrowing power from the Treasury. In other words, the FDIC has approximately 1.2 cents in reserve for every dollar insured. If half of the depositors in the nation demanded their money at one time and the banks couldn't pay it, the FDIC couldn't pay it either.

It's not likely that we're going to see again anything similar to what happened in the 1930s. If I had to wager, I'd bet that in the next 50 years we won't see a run on the banks; but I wouldn't give odds better than five to one against it. It is an unlikely but not inconceivable event.

If depositors as a group get nervous about the stability of the banking system, trouble could ensue. For example, in 1984 the Continental Bank of Chicago (one of the nation's largest banks) was in serious trouble. The bank had made a number of shaky loan decisions, including lending millions of dollars on oil deals that turned sour. These loans became uncollectible. The bank had an unheard-of percentage of outstanding loans that weren't paying interest. As word spread, millions of dollars in large commercial deposits (sometimes called "hot money") were pulled out. This caused other panicked depositors to withdraw their deposits. Finally the FDIC stepped in, guaranteeing all deposits (over $100,000 as well as under) and putting over $1 billion into the bank to rescue it from disaster. As of this writing, the FDIC continues to "put out fires" at banks in the oil belt.

The FDIC's funds are not limitless. If these events continue and accelerate, the system could collapse. In addition, a time bomb is ticking in this direction due to the billions of dollars in perhaps uncollectible loans to South American and other Third World countries that banks still have on their books.

Should an expanded multiple bank run occur, the FDIC couldn't cover all the demands for money, and the banks couldn't liquidate their assets fast enough or at a high enough price to meet depositor demand. You could be the loser.

However, there is a much more pertinent and realistic risk factor in having your money in a bank checking account—the risk of inflation. If you put (*invest*) $100 in your checking account, and if we assume that the annual rate of inflation is six percent, two years later when you take the money out of your account, you can only purchase the equivalent of about $88 worth of goods. You have just lost a lot of purchasing power.

With that $100 investment you are a loser, unless you are earning an interest rate higher than six percent. It is true that you put $100 in the bank and you got $100 back, but when you got it back, the $100 really wasn't worth as much as when you put it in. You have to remember that *money itself isn't wealth.* Real wealth, material wealth, is represented by the things that money will buy. For that reason, inflation is a constant factor, omnipresent in our financial decision making.

Putting your money in a savings and loan institution is similar to putting it in a savings account in a bank. The risks are similar to a bank, in that if there's no general panic, and if your particular savings and loan institution is mismanaged and goes bankrupt, then you won't have any problem getting back the money you invested up to your $100,000 limit. These accounts are insured by another federal agency, the Federal Savings and Loan Insurance Corporation (FSLIC).

Is there a greater risk of a mass run on savings and loan institutions than there is on banks? The risks are different. Savings and loans tend to have a lot of deposits from smaller depositors. Although banks also have many small depositors, they have some very large depositors as well and tend to have more "hot" money, that is, large amounts of money that shift rapidly from one institution (such as other banks or U.S. government notes) to another (à la Continental).

On the other hand, banks are more "liquid," meaning it's easier to get investments converted into ready cash. This means that they invest much of your money in government bonds, municipal bonds and short-term loans that are paid off every six months or every year, whereas savings and loans institutions primarily lend money on home mortgages, which are loans that might extend for as long as 20 or 25 years. Therefore, savings and loan institutions are not very flexible or liquid, and their biggest risk isn't the possibility of a run by depositors as much as the risk of a nationwide collapse in the value of real estate.

If there were a tremendous reduction in the value of homes causing a rash of foreclosures, savings and loan institutions would not receive interest on all their mortgage loans and might in turn have trouble paying interest to their depositors. At that point depositors might start withdrawing funds en masse and the savings and loans would have trouble coming up with the cash for all those withdrawals. But then again, they *are* insured.

Deregulation has resulted in new risks at savings and loans. Several entrepreneurs have used individual savers' deposits to invest in speculative real estate and securities deals. As a result, the reserves of the FSLIC are being depleted as the agency bails out depositors where the "entrepreneur-banker" has made poor investments, putting the savings and loan into government hands to avoid default. There are presently large numbers of insolvent savings and loans still operating in the oil belt and elsewhere. While their liabilities exceed their assets, the FSLIC simply does not have the funds to take them all over. Where this will lead is uncertain, but if massive inputs of funds are required, it will likely come from you in the form of taxes to support this bleeding system until it gets on its feet.

There are advantages to putting your money in cash, i.e., into banks or savings and loans. The main advantage is liquidity: You can convert your savings account or your checking account to cash in an instant; that is, you can simply walk into the institution and get your cash. The second advantage is in the safety of the principal: If you put $100 in a savings account or a checking account, you know that in two months, six months or a year, you'll get your cash back (assuming the system survives). You do run the risk of inflation, but at least in absolute dollars you get your money back. So *safety* and *liquidity* are the incentives for putting your money in these institutions. Anyone with investments who doesn't have some of it in cash that is available immediately if it is ever needed is probably unwise. Despite all the scary talk of bankruptcy of these systems, they are federal agencies and the U.S. government still has the power to print money.

Very Near Cash—Money Market Funds

From the folks who brought us mutual funds (a subject covered later in this book) came a new vehicle that has revolutionized banking: money market funds.

Until the late 1970s, banks and savings and loans were restricted by the government to paying 5.5 percent interest on basic savings accounts. At the same time (1978-79), they were earning interest at rates up to three times that. Along came someone with an inventive idea. Professional money managers gathered money from investors, placed it in U.S. government notes and in short-term notes (IOUs) of blue-chip corporations such as General Electric or General Motors, earning interest rates of nine percent to ten percent. They then gave investors the right to take out their money whenever they wanted (like a bank). It was done through the mail and by phone. Investors kept the full interest earned, less only a small service fee of up to 0.25 percent. These vehicles, termed "money market funds," were as liquid as checking accounts, but earned much higher rates.

Banks and savings and loans tried to hold onto deposits in part by saying, "Those guys aren't insured, as we are. You could lose." This tactic didn't stop the flow of funds from these institutions to the new funds. The number of money market funds continues to grow (see Figure 2.1), and now money market funds outside of banks and savings and loans represent over $200 billion in assets.

There are now hundreds of money market funds to choose from. They can be broken down into three basic types: 1) those that invest in corporate notes; 2) those that invest in U.S. government notes; and 3) those that invest in municipal notes.

The highest rates are paid by the corporate funds, second highest by the U.S. government note funds and the lowest by

FIGURE 2.1   Growth of Money Market Funds

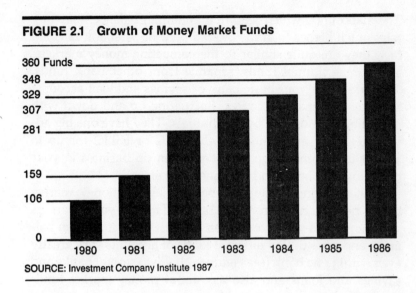

SOURCE: Investment Company Institute 1987

the municipal note funds. Income from the last is free from federal income tax, while income from U.S. notes funds is free from state income tax. Corporate funds, which are fully taxed, have a little more risk and pay one percent to two percent higher interest than funds which invest exclusively in U.S. government securities.

It pays to shop funds. Within each of these categories, rates and service costs may vary. Keep in mind that the safest is a fund that invests in U.S. government securities; since there is no FDIC or FSLIC insurance, safety of where the fund invests is more important than where an insured bank puts your dollars.

The Banks Retaliate

Banks and savings and loans did not like to see depositors withdraw savings and put them in money market mutual funds. Following government deregulation, banks and savings and loans set up their own so-called money market accounts.

These accounts, which require a minimum balance, may pay rates much higher than the old 5.5 percent passbook rates; in fact, they are quite similar to the competing money markets. They aren't mutual funds, separate from other bank funds. They are really your basic bank or savings and loan accounts that pay higher interest rates, fluctuating up and down with prevailing rates offered by the mutuals. They have one big advantage: They are insured by the FDIC or FSLIC for up to $100,000. Another edge is that you can do business in your home town rather than by phone or mail.

There is much more to be said about money market funds, but you now know the basics. The rest you'll learn as you shop—and you *should shop*. Interest rates, minimum balances and penalties on different kinds of accounts vary greatly even within one bank (see Figure 2.2). Go to several banks and savings and loans and also ask about money market funds available through your stockbroker. Compare minimum deposits, maintenance fees, number of free checks, interest rates, safety (insured vs. not, U.S. government vs. corporate notes, etc.) and hassle factors. Then choose which fits your pocketbook and temperament best.

Near Cash—Certificates of Deposit

A certificate of deposit (CD) is a frozen savings account at a bank or savings and loan. It cannot be withdrawn without a penalty for a specified period of time, from three months to 20 or more years. Most typical are six-month to three-year CDs requiring a minimum deposit of $500 to $1,000. The advantage of CDs over other bank accounts is they pay higher interest rates. Also, you are guaranteed that high rate for a long time, whereas money market rates fluctuate weekly. CDs also are insured for up to $100,000. The customary penalty for early withdrawal is reduction of the interest rate on the entire account from the stipulated higher rate to a lower rate or a three to six months' interest penalty. (However, you should read the

FIGURE 2.2   Interest Rates Paid at a Chicago Bank 8/31/87

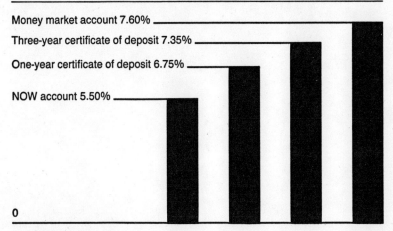

Money market account 7.60%

Three-year certificate of deposit 7.35%

One-year certificate of deposit 6.75%

NOW account 5.50%

0

Money market account
Interest-bearing checking account; $1,000 minimum balance, $15 charge if balance falls below $500, limit of three checks per month except to withdraw cash.

Three-year certificate of deposit
$1,000 minimum balance, penalty of three-months' interest if withdrawn before maturity.

One-year certificate of deposit
$1,000 minimum balance, penalty of three months' interest if withdrawn before maturity.

NOW account
Interest-bearing checking account; $2,500 minimum balance.

fine print before buying a CD.) If you have a sum of cash you know you won't need for quite a while and you are most comfortable dealing with banks or savings and loans, CDs may be well suited for you.

3

Common Stocks

The most common mistake made when investing in the stock market is buying the stock just because the company is a "good" company.

What *Are* Stocks, Anyway?

To facilitate your understanding of a company, its stock and how it works, let's look at an example. Let's go back in time to 1947. Your name is Mr. Land, you're an inventor and you've come up with a terrific idea.* You've been working in your lab for days on end and have just invented a camera that develops its own picture right inside the camera, in just one minute! You don't have to trek to the store, give the clerk your prints and wait a week to get them back. Of course, your camera, which you call "Polaroid," is crude; and sometimes the pictures don't come out too well, but still it's very exciting. You've been to a patent attorney and you now have a patent on your process.

---

*Although this story is based on the Polaroid Corporation, it is simplified for the purpose of example. It is not meant to be factual in terms of exact figures, dates or the depiction of processes or characters.

And then you start thinking, "Gee, I could make a lot of money if I could market this product and sell it to the general public." You sit down with an accountant and talk it over. You realize that you're going to have to build a plant and hire some people to help you, and by the time you're through adding up what your bills will be just to get started, it comes to $1 million. That's a lot of money, but you have confidence in your plan. You don't know much about business and finance, but you think it should be easy to get the money to build your plant. After all, you've got a terrific invention with a lot of potential.

The next morning you wake up and go down to the bank where you have your checking account. You ask to see the president because you know you've got something very important to say. You show him all your figures, your patent and the Polaroid camera. The banker is impressed and asks, "What do you want from me?" You say, "I'd like $1 million. I think I've got a terrific invention that can make millions and millions of dollars and I'm willing to pay you 12 percent interest on your loan, just like you charge everybody else."

The banker chuckles and says, "Mr. Land, why should I lend you $1 million? You see, I only lend money to people when I feel I can't lose. People come in here and say, 'Lend me $1 million, and I'll tell you what, I'll put up $1 million worth of gold, or $2 million worth of diamonds,' and if they don't pay their loan back, I have security. Merchants come in here and say, 'Lend me $1 million so that I can stock my department store this year and everything I sell will go to you until I repay you the $1 million and then I'll keep the remainder.' Again, I have security.

"What I'm saying, Mr. Land, is that I think you have a terrific idea, and I think you *might* make a lot of money, but then again, you might *not*. And people might not accept the Polaroid camera—particularly at the very high price of $300 per camera, which you'll have to charge because of your high cost of development and production. Look at it this way, Mr. Land, if your camera doesn't make it—and there's a chance it won't—we stand to lose our entire $1 million. After all, the only security we get is your patent. Well, we also get the plant as security, but a camera-making plant isn't worth much if it can't make profitable cameras. On the other hand, if you are successful, you're going to make millions and millions of dollars, and we only make 12 percent. So, as I see it, we have a 50–50 chance of losing our entire $1 million or a large part of it, and if we win and you're successful, we only make 12 percent on our money. A bank is not in business to take that kind of risk. Good luck and goodbye, Mr. Land."

Well, of course you are depressed. You walk down the street, your hands in your pockets, feeling frustrated and sorry for yourself. You grumble some angry words to yourself about the banker. But then, the more you think about it, the more you realize that the banker made an obvious and probably intelligent decision. Banks aren't in the business of making loans to people if they have only a *chance* of recouping their investment.

As you walk down the street, you look up and see a sign that says "Merry, Pynch, Fierce, Benner & Dean, Stockbrokers and Investments." You shrug your shoulders and saunter in. You ask to talk to the manager, and you describe your invention to her. The manager is skeptical until you take her picture. Suddenly the manager's much more attentive and introduces you to Mr. Pynch, the president of the stockbrokerage company. Now you learn how you are going to raise the $1 million.

Mr. Pynch makes you an offer: "Well, Mr. Land, first you're going to have to incorporate."

"What does that mean?" you ask.

"That means," answers Mr. Pynch, "that you're going to have a lawyer draft some papers to start something called the "Polaroid Corporation." You put your patent and your invention into the Polaroid Corporation and we'll put money into it, and then if we lose no one can sue us for anything more than is in the corporation. No one can sue us personally. The only one who is liable is this entity, the Polaroid Corporation."

"Wait a minute, Mr. Pynch. Who is going to put money in Polaroid Corporation?"

"Listen carefully, Mr. Land. Here is what we're going to do. We'll print a million pieces of paper that each say, 'Polaroid Corporation, one share of common stock.' We'll get a big metal box and we'll write on it the words 'Polaroid Corporation.' Into that box we'll put these million pieces of paper and—I'll tell you what—you take your patent that you have in your pocket there, put it in the box, Mr. Land, and in exchange for that patent, Polaroid Corporation will give you half a million (500,000) pieces of paper. This means that you will own half the Polaroid Corporation, because only one million shares exist. Each share is worth one-millionth of the corporation. You put the patent in the corporation and in exchange you get half the ownership.

"However, you see, Mr. Land, there's still 500,000 shares sitting in the metal box and we're going to trade those 500,000 shares for the $1 million in cash you need. We're going to go to our customers at Merry, Pynch, Fierce, Benner & Dean and offer them these shares for $2 each. We'll say, 'For $2 you can own one share in the Polaroid Corporation, a company that's going to manufacture these wonderful cameras.' We think we'll be able to find enough investors who want to buy these shares at $2 each to sell all 500,000 shares. Now, you'll have a lot of partners in your business, Mr. Land, but you'll still own half the business, because you own 500,000 shares. The people who each pay us $2 will own one share in your company, or one-millionth of your company."

"I see, Mr. Pynch, but how do you make money on this deal?"

"Well," says Mr. Pynch, "I said I'd charge the people $2 a share for Polaroid. That was a little understated. I would really charge them $2.20 for every share. I'll keep the 20 cents as my fee for each share that I sell and $2 will go into your treasury."

You and Mr. Pynch shake hands. You've made a deal.

One week later, Mr. Pynch keeps his part of the bargain and gives you a check for $1 million that has to be deposited in the account of Polaroid Corporation. You now own half of a company that has $1 million in cash and a patent for a self-developing camera. You are now in business—along with the owners of those 500,000 shares.

The process I just discussed is called *going public*. Once the customers of Merry, Pynch, Fierce, Benner & Dean have bought up all the 500,000 shares that are offered, there are no more of those shares (called *common stocks*) to be bought from the company. The company has its $1 million and now goes on about its business. From this point on, the value of those shares is determined by what other people who would like to own a share in the company are willing to pay these customers for their shares. Henceforth, the company receives no additional monies when the stock is bought and sold. If the fortunes of the company rise, more than likely the price people are willing to pay for a share in the company will also rise.

Today, when you buy a share of Polaroid, you're not buying it from the company. You're buying it from someone who bought it from someone, etc., who 36 years ago bought it directly from the company. Presently, Polaroid is bought and sold on the New York Stock Exchange, where, along with the American Stock Exchange, the sale and purchase of the stocks of most major U.S. corporations take place daily. If you want to buy Polaroid stock today, you would walk into a stockbroker's office in Boston, San Francisco, Water Falls, Iowa or wherever *you* are, and tell the stockbroker you'd like to buy stock. The stockbroker will call his or her representative in New York and ask the representative to buy the stock for you at the best price possible. If you own the stock and want to sell it, you would use the same procedure. The stockbroker charges a commission for this service varying from 0.5 percent to 3.0 percent, whether you're buying or selling. As you can see, Polaroid Corporation itself isn't involved in this transaction at all.

The New York Stock Exchange is where the larger corporations in the United States trade their stock. The American Stock Exchange, the second largest exchange, operates in an identical manner, but tends to trade in somewhat smaller corporations. And the smallest corporations, as well as companies that recently have gone public, tend to be traded in the over-the-counter market. The over-the-counter market isn't a place; it's a loose network of stockbrokers who contact each other by telephone and/or computer to buy and sell stock for their customers. For example, if Company X went public last year and you think that the stock is selling for less than it's worth and you want to buy some, you would tell your stockbroker what you're willing to pay for it. Then your stockbroker would find out which stockbroker in this country specializes in buying and selling that stock. He would call the representative on the phone and negotiate the best possible price for you, again charging you a commission for his trouble.

Let's go back now to our example of Mr. Land and the Polaroid Corporation and figure out what determines the value of a common stock. Let us say that with the $1 million deposited in the account of Polaroid Corporation, Mr. Land sets up shop in 1949. He spends $750,000 to build the plant and keeps the remaining $250,000 in the bank. He then starts taking orders from drugstores and department stores around the country for the cameras. In the next year, 1950, Mr. Land sells a few cameras at $300 each, with final sales totaling $100,000. But since it costs money to sell and produce the cameras (he has workers to pay, sales representatives, and, of course, heat and electricity for the factory), the company spent $200,000. That means Mr. Land lost $100,000.

Now, let's stop and think at this point, what's that stock worth? What is one share of Polaroid worth? If you bought that stock at $2 from the company on the day it went public, and here we are in 1950 and the company lost $100,000, your one share lost one-millionth of that. In other words, your share lost ten cents last year. If someone offered you $2 now for your stock, would you take it? Well, think it over for a while and we'll come back to it.

The year is now 1951. Sales have picked up a lot. Polaroid Corporation has sold $400,000 worth of cameras this year. But costs have gone up to $400,000 also, because it costs more to make more cameras. So this year the company breaks even. At this point some may say that the stock is worth less than it was the day you bought it for $2, because, well, the company lost $100,000 the year before and made nothing this year. Let's look at what the company now owns, its *assets:* a plant worth $750,000 and cash in the bank amounting to $150,000 (down from the original $250,000 due to last year's $100,000 loss). So now the company's total net worth equals $900,000 ($750,000 + $150,000) and there are 1 million shares. Therefore, each shareholder has 90 cent worth of assets in the company, plus each shareholder owns one one-millionth of that patent, which, to make things simple, is worth $1 million or $1 a share. So if a share was worth $2 when you bought it, now it's worth $1.90—in strict asset terms, that is.

Now it is 1952, and the company's fortunes have continued to improve. The Polaroid camera is beginning to catch on and the sales total $1 million. The expense of heating the plant, of supplying the electricity and the salaries for the workers and sales representatives are up to $700,000 this year. But since sales have increased from $400,000 to $1 million, while expenses increased by only $300,000 (costs last year were $400,000), this means that sales are going up at a faster rate than costs. This year the company shows a $300,000 profit. But because there *is* a profit, the company has to pay a *corporate income tax*—in this case, for example, it's $100,000— leaving a $200,000 *net profit*. Well, this means that if you own a share in the company, you earn one-millionth of what the company earns. So your share earns 20 cents. If you owned the whole company, you would have earned $200,000.

Again, I pose the question: What is this share worth? Well, if we add 20 cents to the $1.90 from last year, we would say the share is worth $2.10. Would you pay $2.10 for a share of this stock at this point? Would you sell it for this price? And there's another factor to consider: growth. You might think, "Gee, if the company had sales of $100,000 three years ago, $400,000 last year and $1 million this year, what will it have next year? If the company earned 20 cents for my share of stock this year, how much will it earn next year?"

Of course, the fact that your share earned 20 cents doesn't necessarily mean that you actually receive 20 cents. The directors of the company have to make a decision about what to do with the profits. They can take the money and reinvest it in the company or they can distribute it to you and the other shareholders in the form of *dividends*. Very few corporations, however, distribute all of their earnings in the form of dividends. The more rapidly a company grows, the less the directors tend to distribute in dividends, because they earn so much more money for you by reinvesting it in the company's own growth.

In 1953 the Polaroid Corporation continued to grow. Sales were $3 million and expenses were $2 million; therefore, the company made $1 million in profits. Uncle Sam took one-half of this profit in corporate income tax; so, after taxes, Polaroid made $500,000 or 50 cents a share. Again this year the company pays no dividends, because the directors want to reinvest the earnings to facilitate growth. The cash assets of the company have thus grown by $500,000 or 50 cents a share this year to a total of $2.60 a share ($2.10 + $.50).

Well, let's see what happens in 1954. The company's sales are now $10 million, and the costs are $7.2 million. Therefore, there is a profit of $2.8 million. Again, one-half of that profit goes to Uncle Sam, leaving a net profit of $1.4 million. The company is now earning $1.40 a share, although in terms of *book value* or what the stock is worth in light of assets, if you add $1.40 to the $2.60 it reached last year, the stock is now worth $4 a share. But the earnings make it worth a lot more than that, even if the money is being reinvested, i.e., not paid to you immediately. You'd certainly pay more than $4 to earn $1.40 each year—after all, that's a 35 percent rate of return. As we are about to see, stock values are determined primarily by *earnings per share*, not by the assets per share a corporation possesses.

Earnings per Share Revisited

The concept of earnings per share is vital to understanding stocks, so let's pause and make sure it's understood.

If a corporation has net income of $1 million after expenses and taxes and it was owned entirely by the Happy Family, then they would have made $1 million. They can leave that money sitting in the corporate vault down at the office, use it in corporate investments to help the corporation grow or pull some or all of it out to put in their personal bank account. The latter is called "paying a dividend." If they do pay themselves a dividend, then they have to pay personal income tax on that dividend; that's called "double taxation." First the corporation pays taxes on profits and then those who receive dividends pay personal tax on the dividends.

Now if the company had one million shares of which 999,999 were owned by the Happy Family and one by you, you would have earned $1. Why? Well, you divide

$$\frac{\$1,000,000 \text{ dollars profit}}{1,000,000 \text{ shares}} = \$1 \text{ earnings per share}$$

Whether or not a dividend is declared and part of that $1 million profit is distributed, your share of profits is $1.

If the same company had ten million shares and you owned one of them, your earnings per share would be ...? If they had 100,000 shares, your earnings per share would be ...? Now that you've mastered this key concept, let's move on to the multiplier. (P.S. Answers are ten cents and ten dollars.)

A Look at the Real Polaroid Corporation

It all began during the 1920s at Harvard. Edwin Land, then a student, was investigating in and experimenting with light polarization. At a Harvard colloquium in 1932, the young genius announced he had developed a means of producing a low-cost polarizing material. By 1934 he had received a basic patent for a sheet polarizer.

In 1937 Land formed the Polaroid Corporation to develop light polarization technically and commercially.

In 1937 sales were $147,000; by 1941 sales had grown to $1 million, selling such products as polarized sunglasses.

The company grew 16-fold—to $16 million—during World War II because of military applications. But it wasn't until 1948 that Polaroid got on the track to becoming a major corporation. In that year its instant photography camera was introduced to the consumer and was an immediate smash.

Polaroid became a public corporation in 1957 in order to raise money to expand and began trading on the New York Stock Exchange. By 1977 sales had reached $1 billion. Sales in 1986 were $1.6 billion.

The stock earned 95 cents a share in 1968 and hit a price of $73 per share in the same year (76 times earnings). In 1984 the company earned $1.67 per share and sold at an average price of $30.

Even though Polaroid has come upon hard times because of a decline in consumer interest in instant photography, that stock of Mr. Land and his family are still worth over $100 million.

Source: Polaroid Corporation: A Chronology, Value Line, March 29, 1985

The Multiplier or Price-Earnings Ratio

What is the relationship between a stock's earnings per share and what you pay for it? To figure this out, you must understand the concept of the *multiplier*. The multiplier is indicative of the quality of stocks, just as meat prices reflect the quality of the meat. If a filet mignon weighs three pounds and sells for $4 per pound, and a package of ground chuck weighs three pounds but sells at $1 per pound, even though they both weigh the same, the filet sells for $12 and the ground chuck for $3.

Similarly, if two stocks both earn the same amount per share—let's say $3—one stock may sell at $60 while the other may sell for only $15. The reason for this disparity revolves around how people often view the quality of those earnings. The main determinant of quality in stocks is the expected growth in the future and the growth experienced in the past. Although with meat the measure of quality is the price per pound, with stocks the yardstick of quality is the multiplier, often called "the price-earnings ratio" or the "P/E ratio." As you will see later, the essence of my suggested stock strategy is for you to be able to predict growth, to sniff out and to buy stocks which look like and are priced like ground chuck, but which will later prove to be filets mignons in disguise.

Simply stated, the multiplier is what you get if you divide the market price of the stock by the earnings per share. So, if a stock is currently trading at $60 per share and earned $10 per share last year, its multiplier is six.

$$\frac{\$60}{\$10} = 6$$

You are paying six times earnings for your share of that company. If the stock were selling for $100, you would be paying ten times earnings; at $200, 20 times earnings per share. The more rapidly a company is growing, the higher this multiplier will be.

In the past 25 years, for companies that grow no more rapidly than the economy (three to four percent a year), a rough estimate of the multiplier investors have paid is ten times the annual earnings. In other words, if a company earned $1.40 a share and was expected to grow about as fast as our entire economy, but no faster, you might expect to pay about $14 per share. That's a ten percent return, but it doesn't mean that you would get that return in cash, because, again, the company might retain a good deal of those earnings to reinvest so the company can grow with the use of your money. But the more rapidly people expect a company to grow, the higher the price they'll pay for a share. Price-earnings ratios for the stock market as a whole from 1950–1987 are shown in Figure 3.1.

Let's compare two companies that are both earning $1.40 a share and that have the same asset value per share. One company is Polaroid in the year 1954; it's growing very rapidly. The other is a wholesale grocery business that has been growing at the rate of about one percent a year for the past 15 years. The grocery company is paying a dividend of $1 per share out of its $1.40 in earnings and Polaroid is paying no dividend at all. Some people might feel more comfortable owning stock in a company that pays a substantial dividend, and they might rather pay $14 for that share than $14 for a Polaroid share. The vast majority of people, however, would prefer buying a Polaroid share, even at a greater cost, because they believe it will keep growing. It's earning $1.40 now, but if it keeps growing during the next few years at the rate it has been growing, the company could earn $10, $15 or $20 per share. It is for this reason—the anticipation of increased future earnings—that people pay more than ten times the present earnings per share for a company that is expected to grow.

Earnings per share is the most significant bit of information we can glean about common stock. It's the tool we can use in comparing oranges to oranges. *The most common mistake made when investing in the stock market is buying a stock just because the company is a "good" company.* There are numerous incidents of people who bought stock in a company they thought was going to grow, and they were right, but they lost money anyway. They lost money because they didn't have as much information as you do right now—*they didn't know what earnings per share meant.*

Let's say that a stock is earning $1.40 per share this year. It has a bright and exciting future. People bidding up the price of

FIGURE 3.1   Average Price-Earnings Ratios of Common Stocks, 1955–August 1987

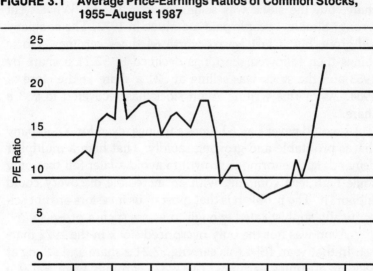

the stock don't understand earnings per share or multipliers; they just know they want to own a share of this exciting company. In the frenzy to own shares, the stock is bid up to $200 per share, or a multiplier of approximately 140 times the earnings per share. Five years later the company is earning $3 per share. It did grow, very nicely in fact, but now the stock is selling at only $100 per share. Even at this price it is selling at 33 times earnings—a higher multiplier than average—indicating that people expect future growth. The buyers of five years ago are now losers. Even though the company has been growing nicely, $200 a share was too much to pay for that future growth. Avon Products is a well-known case in point. In 1972, this door-to-door cosmetics marketer had a record of excellent growth. The years preceding saw earnings of $1.24 per share in 1968, $1.47 in 1969, $1.72 in 1970, $1.89 in 1971 and $2.16 in 1972. In 1972 the stock sold for as much as $139 a share—64

times earnings. By 1979, the company was earning $4.17 a
share, but the stock was selling as low as $38. What went
wrong? Simple—people paid too much in 1972. The company
did grow, but it just wasn't worth 64 times earnings. Worse
things then followed: Earnings declined to $2.21 a share by
1983 and the stock was selling at $21 a share at the close of
1984. As of this writing Avon stock has recovered to $38 a
share.

I would never pay 60 times earnings, even for a company
that is profitable and growing rapidly. That high a multiplier
demands such enormous growth to avoid a later fall that only
some high tech company with an incredible discovery could
support it. The problem is that most of us investors are not sci-
entifically sophisticated enough to assess such a prospect.

Avon was not the only overpriced stock in the 1972 market. In that year, IBM was earning $2.21 a share and selling at
$85, or 40 times earnings. By 1982, earnings were $7.39 a
share, but the stock had gone nowhere—it was selling at $75 a
share or ten times earnings. The IBM story has a happier end-
ing. During 1987 it had reached $175 a share, earning approxi-
mately $10 a share.

The point is this: Every stock has some finite value, no
matter how bright its future. When you pay astronomical multipliers, as people have done during speculative binges, you are
exceeding any reasonable value that can be placed on future
growth and you will later suffer the consequences. Price-
earnings ratios for various industries from 1975-87 are illus-
trated in Table 3.1.

Stock Strategy

My basic investment strategy for dealing with the stock market
has been to find a stock that's both selling at a low multiplier
(less than ten times earnings) and is a growth stock but is not
yet recognized as such by other investors. Say, for example,
that 20 years ago you noticed a little company called Kentucky
Fried Chicken that was earning $1 a share. A fried chicken

TABLE 3.1   Average Price-Earnings Ratios for Industry Groups, 1978–1987

	1978	1979	1980	1981	1982	1983	1984	1985	1986	1987*
Industrials	9.08	8.25	8.26	8.97	9.27	13.78	10.67	13.22	17.71	21.79
Utilities	7.64	7.27	7.17	6.72	6.30	7.34	6.64	8.34	11.08	10.40
Transportation	7.49	6.05	8.67	10.04	13.56	18.79	8.42	12.57	64.21**	108.93**
Financial	6.64	5.83	5.49	6.66	6.52	8.13	10.50	13.86	14.05	10.23
Composite of all S&P 500 Stocks	8.72	7.92	7.98	8.65	6.81	6.98	7.25	12.43	16.45	18.85

*1st Quarter 1987
**In 1986 Transportation stocks lost money in two quarters. Therefore, these P/E ratios are skewed by that event.
Reprinted by Permission of Standard & Poor's Corp.

chain might not have seemed more than moderately promising, but because the stock was selling for only $7 or $8 a share, it seemed like a reasonable investment. Then you tasted their chicken and knew that Kentucky Fried wasn't just ordinary chicken and that, in fact, the business soon would be growing nationwide.

Let's say you bought the stock at $8 a share, and the earnings went from $1 to $10 a share over the next five years. If the multiplier stayed at the same figure (eight times earnings), the stock value would go from $8 a share to $80 a share. You would have done very well.*

But this situation would be compounded by another factor: If, in the eyes of the public, a no-growth company becomes a growth company, people are willing to pay a higher multiplier for the earnings. So instead of paying eight or ten times earnings, people may pay 15 or 20 or even 30 times earnings for a growth company. And now you not only have the advantage of increased earnings per share; you also get the compound benefit of having the market value of your stock increase because people are paying a higher multiplier for those

---

*Figures, facts and dates are for example only and are not meant as factual.

earnings. As a result, when your Kentucky Fried Chicken stock earnings went from $1 to $8, the stock value didn't just go from eight to 80; rather, people started to pay 30 or 40 times earnings for the stock, because they saw it was a growth stock and wanted to buy it before the earnings went even higher. Thus, your stock increased in value from $8 to $240 or more in those few years.

If you buy a stock with a low multiplier your risks are greatly reduced. Your main risk is that the earnings will go down; the multiplier doesn't have much lower to go. (*REMEMBER: The value of the stock is the earnings per share times the multiplier.*) If, on the other hand, you buy a stock with a very high multiplier, for example, at 40 times earnings, you run two risks: that the earnings will go down and that the multiplier will go down. Again: Buy stocks with low multipliers (under ten) that will grow. Avoid high multiplier stocks.

The next section will help you understand this point further.

What's in a Name?

Look at Table 3.2, which will clarify my point by comparing two hypothetical companies. In 1985 both companies had the same earnings per share. Nuclear Computer Growth Technology, Inc. earned $1 and so did Jack's Repair Shops, Inc. Now, Nuclear Computer Growth Technology sounds like a very exciting business. People saw that it was earning $1 per share and although the company had no real history, having been in business for only one year, there were plenty of customers for its stock. After all, it sounded like an exciting, growing field. No one, however, did their research. They didn't know that NCGT was a janitorial service for IBM's office in downtown Tucson, Arizona. The owners in Tucson do, of course, have the right to give their company any name they want. Nuclear Computer Growth Technology sounded so much more exciting than "Tucson Janitorial Service."

TABLE 3.2   Earnings per Share

	Nuclear Computer Growth Technology, Inc.	Jack's Repair Shops, Inc.
1985	$1.00	$1.00
1986	.80	1.80

The second company in the illustration, Jack's Repair Shops, is a company that repairs microcomputers. The name didn't really excite people, so when they saw that this new company was earning $1 per share, they said, "Well, if I pay seven times earnings (or $7 a share) for this stock, that would be a fair price, because if it maintains the same earnings, I'd be making about 14 percent on my money. Fourteen percent is the minimum I want to earn in order to justify taking the risk of buying stock in this kind of dull company that really doesn't look like it has much growth potential."

One year later we see that the Jack's Repair Shops showed earnings of $1.80, up from the $1 for the previous year. The reason is simple: They were in a growth business—the business of repairing computers was growing rapidly along with the sales of computers for the home. The earnings went up 80 percent. The sales grew by 80 percent. People began to look at this stock and say, "Wow! This isn't a dull company; it's a growing company!" And instead of paying seven times earnings, people were willing to pay 25 times earnings. They thought those earnings would grow and that in two or three years they'd really only be paying eight or ten times those earnings. Well, the earnings increased by 80 percent, the multiplier tripled and as a result the stock rose to $45 a share.

If we look at our Nuclear Computer Growth Technology Company, we see that just the opposite happened. Earnings slid from $1 to 80 cents. That's not terrible, but it's not the dynamic growth people were expecting from such a dynamic name. People who owned the stock received the annual report explaining why the earnings went down. They also found out

NCGT was just a janitorial service company, lost interest in it and sold their stock. The stock went from a multiplier of 40 to a multiplier of seven. Then other investors said, "I don't mind paying seven times earnings for a janitorial company that shouldn't grow. If it manages to survive, I'll make a reasonable rate of return on the money if I pay only seven times earnings." As you can see, things can work very dramatically when a growth company stops growing. The multiplier decreased drastically, earnings went down and the stock's market price went from $40 to $5.60 a share.

This illustration points out a very simple fact of life in the stock market. When you buy a stock with a very high multiplier—that is, a stock that people think will grow tremendously—you can make money if the earnings keep growing as rapidly as people expect. *However, if the earnings' growth rate stops, you run the risk of the multiplier falling substantially.* If the earnings should happen to go down, not only do you have the normal effect of the stock going down just because earnings are down, you have the substantial impact caused by both the multiplier and the earnings going down. *In other words, with a high multiplier stock, you stand to lose your shirt.* There are substantial risks with such stocks that don't exist if the stock has a very low multiplier. For one thing, if the multiplier is very low, it can't go much lower. A multiplier of 40 can drop as low as four or five, but a multiplier of five, six or seven just doesn't have much further to go. With stocks with low multipliers you can lose money only on one side of the formula (stock's price = earnings per share × multiplier)—that's with a decrease in earnings.

One of my happiest investment memories is of a stock I bought in 1974. In that year, Community Psychiatric Centers (CPC) was a small over-the-counter company selling at three times earnings. I invested $3,000 in what I thought was a growth company, but the market disagreed. For whatever reason, psychiatric hospitals did not strike the fancy of investors as a growth industry and despite the fact that CPC's earnings had grown 30 percent or 40 percent a year over the four years prior to 1974, it was not yet popular with investors.

I called the president of the company, Mr. Green. He was very comfortable talking with me about the future of the company and laid out the pattern of growth he anticipated. Mr. Green's predictions all came true. The company grew substantially that year and, amazingly, continued to grow every year for ten years. Not only did the multiplier go from three to as high as 26 but earnings grew over 15-fold.

I sold too soon, in 1981, when the stock was selling at 17 times earnings. According to my own investment philosophy, the multiplier was getting a little rich. Well, earnings kept rising and the multiplier never fell. As I write this the multiplier is at 26. That $3,000 investment would today be worth approximately $900,000 (nine times what I received in 1981).

Nothing in investing is utterly and completely simple. In 1962 I met a man who had all his money tied up in stock in Xerox Corporation. At the time the stock was selling at 70 times earnings and he had $50,000 worth of stock. He had bought this stock in 1954 for a $300 total investment. I suggested he sell his stock because he was taking a tremendous risk holding on to a stock at 70 times earnings. If the earnings should decline in any one year, the selling price of the stock could fall 50, 60 or even 80 percent in value when people realized it was not really worth 70 times earnings. Stubbornly, he held on to his stock. I told him he was crazy; he thanked me for my advice and wasn't too offended at my insult.

Ten years later his stock was worth $1 million. I don't think the man really understood the risk he was taking, but he turned out to be right in holding on to the stock. What happened is a story you all know: Xerox had dynamic growth until 1962, at which point it was a large company with sales of approximately $300 million. But it didn't stop there as one might have expected.

In 1972, Xerox had sales of over $2 billion and earnings per share of $3.16. The stock was *still* at 70 times earnings.

What advice would you have given this man in 1972? Had he held on through 1984, he would have been unhappy. Earnings in 1983 came in at $4.35 a share (after peaking at $7.33 in 1980) and the stock was trading at $38. Even though Xerox continued to grow, the stock never again reached the peak 1972 price of $171 a share. Even when the stock earned $7.33 in 1980, the shares sold for $70. In other words, if he held the stock until the end of 1984, his $1 million would have shrunk over 75 percent to $230,000. By 1987 the stock had moved up to $84, commanding a P/E ratio of 19 in an again-excited speculative market. The next section may help you determine when to jump off the track, when a high multiplier is no longer justified.

Predicting Growth

Predicting growth is the name of the game in making money in the stock market. Figure 3.2 shows a pattern of growth that has held true repeatedly for corporations that have grown from small entities into industrial giants. If you look at the growth pattern of General Motors through the 1950s or IBM and Xerox in the late 1950s through early 1970s or Wang (the word processing company) through the 1970s and early 1980s, this pattern keeps recurring. Small corporations struggle in the beginning of their existence, then they go through a period in which they have extremely rapid growth as their product begins to catch on. But it is inevitable that at some point the product will reach a saturation level, and will grow only with growth in the economy. As you see in Figure 3.2, between points A and B when the company is just beginning to get its product known and is learning from its mistakes, growth is slow. Between points B and C is the period of dynamic growth when public acceptance and demand for the product accelerates. The company is expanding its plant, and therefore its capacity to produce, and is realizing an extremely high rate of return on every dollar invested.

FIGURE 3.2   Life Cycle of a Growth Company

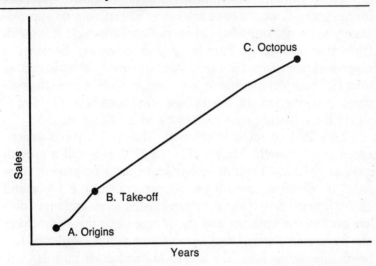

A. **Origins**   Company in founding years (approximately first through fourth years).

B. **Take-off**   Company has completed patents, designs, etc., has learned from previous errors and is ready to fly.

C. **Octopus**   Company has become large, successful corporation and is too big to grow at a dramatic pace.

As an illustrative example, let's look at IBM. During the 1950s and 1960s, when corporations were increasingly converting their bookkeeping operations to data processing systems, IBM enjoyed the dynamic growth that we see in Figure 3.2 between points *B* and *C*. In the 1960s IBM supported a high multiplier, sometimes hitting 60 times earnings. In the 1980s, however, the multiplier was as low as nine. Part of the reason for this decline is that IBM simply can no longer grow at 40 or 50 percent a year. Now, being one of the largest corporations in the world, it's approaching point *C* in Figure 3.2. If it continued to grow at the rate of 40 or 50 percent a year, sooner or later it would be larger than the whole world economy, which can grow at only three or four percent. If IBM grew at 100 percent a year from its present base and kept growing at that pace for ten years, it would have sales over $20 trillion, or approximately ten times our whole gross national product. It is inevitable that sooner or later a growth company becomes a no-growth company. IBM may still be growing at a faster pace than General Motors, but it is no longer truly a growth company. It is entering the third phase, that area beyond point C where there is still growth, but at a much slower rate.

Let's look at another company that recently has experienced great growth: McDonald's. In 1987 is it still a growth company? I'd say it's turning the corner into a no-growth company. Its dynamic growth period occurred in the 1960s and 1970s. It grew in two ways: by franchising more and more outlets around the country and by buying back these franchises and becoming a larger and larger direct public retailer of fast foods. Sooner or later, the fast food hamburger business will reach a saturation point. You simply can't keep growing at 30 to 40 percent a year. As you read this book, I'll bet that you're within a mile of a McDonald's hamburger stand. So ask yourself these questions: "How fast can this company grow?" "How much more room is there for McDonald's stands?" "Can they double next year and have a hamburger stand within a half-mile of my house, and then within a quarter-mile of my house?" The answer is simple: They *can* grow, but not as fast as they used to.

Now I'll give you my formula for getting rich in the stock market. Choose a company whose growth is close to point B in Figure 3.2: A company that is in its infancy and has a product or service that's going to be in tremendous demand, has an ability to deliver that product or service and can do it profitably. Use your common sense, study the information available and, most important, choose a company in which you don't have to pay a huge premium for future growth. Picking such a company requires research, groundwork and a little good luck.

For example, if you see a company at point *B* and you're convinced that this company is going to grow substantially in the next few years, but you have to pay 200 times earnings to buy a share of stock, don't buy. You don't have much to gain, but you do have a lot to lose. Even if the company does what you expect and does grow substantially, the multiplier is unlikely to stay at such a high level. People have already paid for earnings they will receive five years down the road. If you're wrong about the future growth of the company, you'll lose your shirt. You should find a company sitting at point *B* that is selling at a relatively low multiplier—a multiplier that would reflect the fact that most people don't see this as a future growth company.

Getting It All Together

Now we get to an even tougher question: Where do we find companies that are at points *A* and *B*, and that other people might not recognize as likely growth companies? After all, you're reading this book because you don't know much about stocks and investments, so how are you supposed to find companies that even many experts haven't found? I believe that you *can* find these companies. Experts simply don't have the time; they're too busy investing money for wealthy clients in safe companies that are already near the end of their growth pattern. (I'll explain more about that later when we talk about mutual funds.)

To find good investments you must do some research and your research should begin with *The Wall Street Journal*, a daily newspaper, and with *Barron's*, which is sort of a Saturday *Wall Street Journal*.

Acquaint yourself with both of these newspapers. Buy a *Wall Street Journal* and open it up to the section titled "NYSE-Composite Transactions" (New York Stock Exchange). It's usually on the next-to-last page. You'll see a listing of company names and the dividends that these companies pay annually

(See example in Table 3.3). Next to the dividend column will be a column showing the P/E ratios for each company, for example, whether the stock is selling at seven times earnings or 12 times earnings. The earnings referred to are for the last 12 months of the company's operation. Next you'll find the number of shares that were traded yesterday, the high and low price at which each stock sold, the price at which each stock closed and whether the stock went up or down for the day.

If you go back a page you'll find the same listings for the American Stock Exchange, which, as I mentioned earlier, deals in somewhat smaller companies. This section is titled "Amex-Composite Transactions." You'll also see the New York Exchange Bonds and "Over-the-Counter Markets" sections.

Table 3.4 gives an example of an over-the-counter stock. You'll see the dividend that stock pays, and the *bid* and *asked* prices. The *bid* is the price at which people are willing to buy the stock. For example, if the bid is six, it means that someone will pay $6 for a share of a particular stock. The *asked* refers to the price that sellers of the stock have said they will take. The bid is six, but the seller may be holding out for seven. So, it looks like there will be a lot of haggling and, in a sophisticated way, there really will be. If you want to buy the stock, and the bid is six and the asked is seven, you will probably have to pay more than six and less than seven. (See Table 3.4.)

The next step is to find the section titled "Digest of Earnings Reports" (or "Earnings Digest") that's printed every day in *The Wall Street Journal.* (See Table 3.5.) Check the "Today's Index" on the first page to find the page number. Every corporation that is publicly owned, i.e., has stock that you can buy on one of these markets, has to let the public know its financial results every three months. These results are printed in *The Wall Street Journal* every morning. It is helpful to read through these statements *every morning* and look for corporations that have both growth in sales and growth in earnings per share. As you find companies that look interesting to you, check the

TABLE 3.3   Examples from *The Wall Street Journal,* August 25, 1987
From the "New York Stock Exchange" page

52 Weeks		Stock	Div	Yld %	PE Ratio	Sales 100s	High	Low	Close	Net Change
High	Low									
59³/₈	37	Wolwth	1.32	2.3	16	2706	57¹/₂	56¹/₂	56¹/₂	−³/₄

TABLE 3.4   From the NASDAQ Bid and Asked Quotations

Stocks & Div	Sales 100s	Bid	Asked	Net Change
Hospital News	43	6³/₈	6³/₄	−¹/₈

TABLE 3.5   From the "Digest of Earnings Reports"

Year June 27	G & K Services, Inc. (0) 1987	1986
Revenues	$80,755,000	$71,586,000
Net income	4,741,000	3,902,000
Shr earns:		
Net income	1.00	.84
13 weeks:		
Revenues	21,020,000	19,206,000
Net income	1,093,000	844,000
Shr earns:		
Net income	.23	.18

back pages to see what the stocks of these companies are selling for. If a stock is selling at a relatively low multiplier and you think that the company, from the little you know about it, might be a growing company, you should research it further.

The next step is to go to a stockbroker's office and tell the stockbroker that you are interested in knowing more about XYZ Corporation. Ask for a Standard & Poor's sheet on the corporation. (How do you find a stockbroker? Look in the Yellow Pages, and don't be bashful. Most stockbrokers want your business, even a few hundred dollars' worth.) What is the Standard & Poor's sheet? Your stockbroker will show you what that is. Basically, it's one page of information explaining what the corporation does and showing its economic history over the past ten years.

After reading this sheet, the chances are that you'll rule out the XYZ Corporation as a good investment. If you don't decide to look elsewhere, however, the next step is either to buy some shares or—if you have the nerve—to pick up the phone, call an officer of the company and say that you're thinking of investing in the company. Whatever doubts you have about the company's future, share them with the officer. He or she may be rude to you or very helpful. The only thing you have to lose is the cost of the phone call. The smaller the company is, the more likely the officer will be talkative. Owners of businesses, particularly smaller businesses, enjoy talking about them, and very often they're proud of them.

Let's look closely now at Table 3.6. It's a mathematically simple example of what you might find in the "Earnings Digest" in *The Wall Street Journal*. The hypothetical company, Technology Data, Inc., had a growth in sales of $3 million for the quarter ending March 31, going from $7 million in 1986 to $10 million in 1987. (That's a growth rate of about 40 percent.) The earnings grew proportionately. Then we see how the company did for 12 months, ending March 31, 1987. For the whole year sales grew from $28 million to $40 million, which is, again, about a 40 percent growth rate. The earnings grew proportionately: $4 a share, up from $2.80 the year before. You know nothing more than the earnings and the name of the company, but you turn back to the over-the-counter market and look it up. You find that the stock is selling at $26 a share,

TABLE 3.6   Technology Data, Inc. Earnings Report, 1987

	1987	1986
For three months ending March 31:		
Sales (or Revenues)	$10,000,000	$ 7,000,000
Net income after taxes	$ 1,000,000	$ 700,000
Shares outstanding	1,000,000	1,000,000
Earnings per share	$1.00	$.70
For the year ending March 31:		
Sales	$40,000,000	$28,000,000
Net income after taxes	$ 4,000,000	$ 2,800,000
Shares outstanding	1,000,000	1,000,000
Earnings per share	$4.00	$2.80

(When only quarterly earnings are shown, you may estimate for the year by multiplying by four.)

or about 6¹/₂ times present earnings. That seems like a reasonable price or maybe even a very cheap price, so you decide to research it further. You go to your stockbroker and say that you'd like some information on Technology Data, Inc. You get a Standard & Poor's sheet from the stockbroker and read all about the company's history. As you look back on the earnings per share, you find that from 1983 to 1985 the company had no-growth sales of about $28 million and earnings of about $2.80 per share. Its only growth occurred last year. You also discover that it is a national manufacturer and distributor of promotional items for civic groups and a national manufacturer of flags and pennants. It appears that it has done well this year due to the sale of some old flags found in the basement that turned out to be valuable antiques. This disappoints you tremendously; it looks like the reason for this growth is only temporary. By the end of 1987, the company might just be back where it was in 1984 and 1985.

But suppose that you look at Technology Data and find a totally different story. In researching you find that the sales in the past five years have grown from $9 million to $40 million, and that its business consists of a chain of inexpensive cafeterias in two southern states. The company has grown from one restaurant ten years ago to 45 restaurants today. You also find in the report that the company is scheduled to open another 20 restaurants during the next year and that almost every restaurant opened is profitable from the first day of operation.

Now you have reason to be enthusiastic. This looks like a company that will grow. It's in only two states, which leaves lots of room for expansion; it's selling at a low P/E ratio; it's profitable; it's growing rapidly; and for some reason other people don't see it (yet, anyway) as a growth company. At this time you either take your plunge and invest, or you decide to check it out further by calling and trying to talk to an officer of the company.

Suppose you do call and wind up talking to the executive vice-president. You explain that you're interested in investing some of your money in the company and would surely appreciate learning a little about the whole operation—what type of products it offers its customers, what he or she sees as the future of the company, etc. The executive vice-president may say that, in fact, it is opening 20 restaurants next year and that he or she expects they will open at least that many more the year after. In other words, business is good. Now you have one more reason to take the plunge!

On the other hand, if he or she is apprehensive about giving you information or gives you some discouraging news, you would have to reconsider. Apprehension may stem from a fear that might violate some security law by giving you information that isn't already public knowledge, which is a reasonable fear and shouldn't discourage you from investing. But in the area of evaluating the information you get from an officer of the company, there's a lot of intuitive judgment involved. You really have to judge by the tone of the person's voice and manner whether or not you think the person is hiding negative news from you or just being cautious in the information given you. Most officers of companies that are doing well are usually glad to share their enthusiasm with you.

I would suggest that before you call a company officer, write down the questions you want to ask. General questions such as, "Can you tell me about the company and its future?" will not get you very useful information. You would be better off asking more specific questions, such as, "I see you grew by 40 percent last year and that you're planning to open 20 restaurants next year. Do you think you can maintain that rate of growth for more than one year?" Or you might say something like, "There's a lot of competition in this business. Do you feel that you can keep growing at this rate in spite of the stiff competition?" Regarding the answers you get, believe the negatives, weigh the positives and beware of the evasives. It boils down to your subjective evaluation of the information they give you.

Now, assume you've gone ahead and purchased the stock. The next question is, "How long do you hold on to it?" Once again, there's no absolute answer. If the company's stock rises to a multiplier that you consider speculative, you may want to sell. Suppose, for example, you bought a company at six or seven times earnings and were right that, in fact, it was a growth company. If the stock responded appropriately and went to a higher multiplier (for example, 30 to 40 times earnings) with higher earnings, you'd be way ahead of the game, but you might want to take your profit and sell at this point. You've made money by picking a low multiplier growth company that's now become recognized as a growth company by the public. If, on the other hand, you learn a lot about this company's operations and think that it's going to continue growing at an extremely rapid pace (as rapidly as the multiplier reflects or even more rapidly), you may want to hold on to the stock.

But remember, no company grows rapidly forever. You don't want to be married to this stock. You may want to hold on to it for one, three or even five years, but it's very unlikely to be in your interest to hold on to any stock for an indefinite period of time. At some point, when the stock's price reflects your intelligent judgment about its maximum worth, you would be better off selling it and finding another undervalued company in which to invest.

True Growth and "Hyped" Growth

You must be careful to distinguish between *true growth* and phony or *"hyped" growth*. For example, a company's earnings may have doubled last year, but if you do some research and analyze why its profits grew, you may find that it had nothing to do with growth or sales but was due to increased efficiency in its operations. For example, if the sales were the same as the year before, but the profits or earnings per share doubled, it isn't a growth company. If sales don't grow, a company can't show increased profits for very long. Once a company has streamlined its operation so that it makes more for each dollar of sales, from that point on its sales have to increase in order for its earnings to grow. Let's say that for two years in a row a corporation has had sales of $10 million, but it showed profits of $1 million this year versus $500,000 last year. This means it's now making ten cents for every $1 of sales, versus five cents previously. It's unlikely that the company will double its earnings next year (up to 20 cents on every $1 of sales) if it doesn't significantly increase its sales. In fact, very few corporations can make over 15 percent profit on every $1 of sales. *So when you look at a company's quarterly or annual report, you want to look at both growth in earnings per share and growth in sales.*

You also might find a company whose earnings have doubled, not because it sold any more products or delivered any more services, but because of the sale of an asset in the company. Look at company *ABC*, a clothing manufacturer. Its earnings per share doubled this year, although its sales volume stayed the same as last year. What happened? Five years ago ABC purchased a site for possible expansion, but then decided not to expand. This year the company sold the site for a substantial profit over the price it paid five years ago. To accurately assess the company's progress for the year, you must subtract the profit made on that sale from other earnings. The liquidation of an asset is a one-time event.

A similar thing happened in the 1960s when a lot of people were fooled by the temporary growth in earnings of franchise companies. Parent companies selling franchises made a lot of money through the fees they received when they sold their franchises, but they made little or nothing from the actual operations of the franchises. In one year, a company might have sold 200 or 300 franchises and received a fee of $10,000 to $25,000 from each franchisee for the right to do business under its name. In that year, the company showed a great profit. Once the sales of the franchises tapered off, however, and the parent company had to rely on the commissions received from these operations—for which they must also provide services—the parent company no longer made a profit.

In the mid-1960s I bought stock in a company that was franchising family-priced restaurants and selling at $8 a share. I thought this was a pretty good price because the year I bought the stock the company earned $1 a share, whereas the year before the company had earned only about 40 cents a share, and the year before that about ten cents a share. The public responded the way I hoped and quickly drove the stock up to $40 a share. People saw this as a fantastic growth company and were therefore willing to pay 40 times earnings, based on the assumption that in two or three years the company would be earning $3 to $4 a share and the stock would be doing fine. When I looked back and analyzed why this company had grown so much, I found that almost all of its profits were from the sale of franchises to franchisees. Its other activities, including earnings from continuing operations of its own restaurants and royalties from franchises that were in operation (it also was collecting around four percent of sales from its franchisees), weren't profitable at all. In order to make money, it would have to continue selling franchises. But by then there was a slack in the economy. No one wanted to buy the franchises, and investors had to look to the basic operation of the company to find the true value of the stock.

Fortunately for me, I needed cash and sold the stock at $32. A year later it was selling for less than $1 a share, because the company was no longer earning money and, in fact, was running at a deficit of around ten cents a share. Sixteen years have passed since then; the stock is now selling for about $2 a share.

A much easier trap to fall into is investing in a company that has shown significant growth for one or two years based solely on profitable operations, but whose growth is founded on something that isn't going to last. For example, if you bought stock in the corporation that produced this year's biggest box office hit, you should have been careful not to pay a high multiplier. Even worse would be to pay a multiplier that would reflect the optimistic assumption that this company will come out with two movies like this next year and four the year after.

Sales per Share

Another useful tool to determine if a stock is over- or undervalued is *sales per share*, which is derived by dividing a corporation's total sales by the total number of shares. For example, if a corporation has $100 million in sales and one million shares outstanding, its stock has $100 in sales per share.

In the rush to merge and acquire in the 1980s, the buyout candidates typically have been selling at bargain levels by this yardstick.

One yardstick in buying a private (or public) corporation is: How big is the business? The larger the sales, the bigger the business, and the bigger the price tag it will command.

A useful benchmark for value is one times sales. A company with $100 million in sales, if profitable, may sell at $100 million. Why? If a company has a healthy profit margin, i.e., converts sales to profits, it may keep from three percent to 15 percent of every dollar of sales as after-tax profits. If, let us say, it keeps 8½ percent, then it makes $8.5 million. What would a buyer of going companies pay for such an ongoing business? If the company is growing, a buyer may pay from $75 million to $125 million because that buyer hopes to keep increasing the earnings and would be paying between nine and 12 times present earnings.

If the stock for a corporation with $100 in sales per share were selling for $300 a share, it would be a signal that you're paying a very rich price (three times sales). If it's selling at $25 a share, it's a signal that it may be cheap.

When stocks sell at a small fraction of sales per share (say one-fifth of sales) the company is probably not converting its sales dollars to profit dollars. If through cost cutting, new marketing or whatever, those sales can be made profitable, the company and its stock could be worth one times sales or more.

Many shrewd buyers of corporations, called "corporate raiders," have been buying corporations which are bargains, based on sales; they then convert those huge sales to huge profits and see the worth of their newly acquired companies soar. In 1987 Carl Ichan saw TWA follow this pattern. He purchased a troubled airline (or at least a big chunk of the airline) at a small fraction of total sales, made the losing company profitable and saw the stock he originally purchased at as low as $14 per share soar to $38 at this writing.

I have recently bought shares of two other airline stocks that fit the pre-TWA takeover mold, Texas Air and Air Midwest. Texas Air, trading on the American Stock Exchange, is selling at $27 a share, down from a high of $51 a share. Texas Air is the minnow that swallowed the whale. In 1986 it purchased Eastern Airlines and then People Express. It did not increase the shares in its company, but borrowed billions to make the purchases. That made it a more risky company because it then had a huge monthly interest debt, but on the other hand, this made it look very cheap in terms of sales per share. For every share of stock, Texas Air generates $190 of sales.

Let's look at the up side—how much could this stock go up from $27? If, let us say, airline ticket prices increase and they continue to fill 70 percent to 75 percent of their seats (breakeven used to be at 50 percent occupancy when fares were higher), and that this results in an eight percent profit margin on sales, the stock could earn $15 a share. Applying what we have learned about P/E ratios, if the public attaches a P/E of ten times earnings, the stock would sell at $150. If the public became really enthusiastic, the stock could sell as high as $200. Another interesting aspect of this low price-to-sales ratio (15 percent) is the possibility that a corporate raider would be attracted to this situation and offer a higher price than $27 to buy the entire company. The most likely raider at this time would be Frank Lorenzo, the head of the company.

Air Midwest is a much smaller commuter airline. Recently I noticed that its stock had gone down from $11 a share to 2⅝. I also noticed that it had about $15 in sales per share. I called the company, asked for its annual report, read it and was convinced that this was an opportunity. The company had been losing money, but was turning things around. By the time I decided to buy the stock, one week after my initial interest, the stock had risen to 4¼. I discerned that the company should have about $19 in sales per share in 1987 and that at 4¼ it was still a good buy. I bought stock in the company, which is now trading at 5¾. The company is making money and I am estimating that for 1987, it may make a profit of as much as $1.25 a share.

It may be an informative and fun exercise for you to put down the book at this point, open The Wall Street Journal to the "Over-the Counter Markets" section and the American Stock Exchange, and see if the sales of these companies have been converted to high profits. If the stock prices are much higher you will know they have become more profitable. If the stocks are much lower, either the overall stock market has tumbled to more "reasonable" levels, the public believes these companies won't convert their sales to big profits, or fear in an economic downturn they'll go broke.

This tool, sales per share, is useful to combine in your research. Look for bargains, i.e., stocks selling at one-quarter or one-third of sales per share, that you think may be likely to convert their low-profit or no-profit sales to big profits. If the sales are also growing rapidly, you may have the potential for huge profit.

Low-Risk Stock Investments

Perhaps you're reading this book to learn how to invest in companies without a lot of risk—companies that you think of as solid and substantial, like General Motors, Proctor & Gamble or Sears. You know now where they fit on the growth curve and that large corporations which have reached their full maturity may be sound investments. They may be sound, but they're not going to make you rich.

If you understand the game of investing in small growth companies, you shouldn't have much trouble with large companies on the New York Stock Exchange. The rules of the game are very similar. When you invest in a large corporation you don't want to pay an inappropriately high multiplier for the present earnings. From time to time you will even find large corporations that are selling at bargain levels because their multipliers are inappropriately low. A few years ago, for example, Kresge was selling at a low multiplier. It looked like a company that had very little growth left; the dime store business didn't look very promising. Then it opened K mart, and a rapid rate of growth followed. Even though Kresge was a large corporation 15 years ago, you still could have made substantial profits by buying the stock then, when its low multiplier reflected the company's poor prospects, and by selling the stock today when both the earnings and the multiplier are significantly higher.

However, the Kresge/K mart story is not typical. As a rule, large mature companies will reach the end of the growth cycle, taper off and never experience another period of accelerated growth as Kresge did. Big does not necessarily mean safe. Xerox, as you now know, was a multibillion dollar blue-chip investment in 1972, but the stock fell 75 percent over the next 12 years, before it returned to favor. People who said you can't lose by buying steel and auto stocks in the 1960s and early 1970s were dead wrong. Most of these safe, solid, blue-chip stocks slid dramatically and took 15 years to recover, if they recovered at all.

If your broker says a stock is safe, that it's a solid blue-chip stock, you'd best think for yourself. They've been wrong, as you can see, many times before. In the end, you must think for yourself to succeed.

4

The Forest for the Trees

Don't get caught up in the euphoria or the doom and gloom that may surround you. Know your rules, trust them and trust yourself.

Common stocks are sometimes a wonderful investment and at other times a poor investment. There is a tendency for all common stocks to move together in price, a kind of magnet effect. When the stock market is going up, most stocks go up; when the stock market is going down, most stocks go down. The way to deal with this is simple. When stocks in general are selling at prices that are unjustified (the market is too high), don't buy. Sell. When the market is selling at bargain prices and stocks are lower than the realities of the business situation justify, you should buy.

One way to find out when the market has reached its top or bottom is to talk to ten stockbrokers. When ten stockbrokers think that now is a good time to buy stocks, it's probably *not* a good time. Conversely, if they're all sure that this is the worst possible time, because the market is going straight down, then it's a good bet that now's the time to buy.

Of course I'm being sarcastic, but what I'm getting at is that euphoria begets euphoria and doom and gloom beget the same doom and gloom. When the stock market has gone up for a period of time, brokers see many happy customers. They can point to the profits being made and so it's easier for them to be enthusiastic. When the markets have been going down for several months, however, or for a year or two, they don't feel too good about what they have to offer. Thus, it's harder for them to say with a smile, "Yes, you should be buying stock."

One way of finding out when the stock market is too high or too low is to study the price-earnings ratio on the New York Stock Exchange. The Dow Jones Industrial Average is a figure derived from 30 large companies. A complicated formula adds the value of 30 stocks together and then divides by a certain number. The figure is used as a barometer for the condition of the entire stock market. Over the past 25 years these stocks have sold for prices that ranged from about five times earnings to about 18 times earnings.

Another excellent index, and one which is more broadly based, is the Value Line Investment Survey, covering approximately 1,700 stocks. The average multiplier (or P/E ratio) for these stocks in the past 20 years has been as low as 4.8 in 1974 and as high as 19.0 in 1968. At the end of August 1987, it stood at 16.9 times earnings.

1974: A Case in Point

In 1974, the Dow Jones Industrial Average had fallen to 580, down from its 1971 high of 1,050. The market price of these stocks had declined tremendously, about 45 percent in value. At 580 the Dow Jones Industrial Average was selling at less than six times earnings and, as we noted, the Value Line Index at less than five times earnings. Smaller company shares traded on the American Stock Exchange and in over-the-counter markets were frequently selling at only two, three and four times annual earnings. At that point very few stockbrokers pushed their customers to buy stock. For two or three years people had seen the value of their stock holdings decline. Most who followed the stock market at all or who owned stocks were very pessimistic about the market and the most common words of wisdom were, "Stay away from the stock market; it's a terrible place to invest." It's not surprising that people felt negative about the stock market, and the more negative they felt the more they kept selling their stocks. The small investors weren't the only ones selling their stock; money managers, bankers and people in charge of trust funds were also selling. They were tired of losing money, so they sold their stocks and put more of their assets in cash. Thus, the more people sold their stocks, the lower the stocks went, because flooding the market with stocks drives the price down.

There was a lot of doom and gloom and many reasons to be unhappy about the economy. Inflation was running at 12 percent, unemployment was increasing and the oil embargo was raising costs of petroleum products dramatically. Moreover, stocks were selling at such low price-earnings ratios, it was as if there was a message, "If you think things are bad now, just wait until tomorrow!" There were examples galore of this sort of depression mentality. In some cases, stocks were selling for prices as low as two or three times earnings while yielding dividends of ten percent or 12 percent. Other stocks were selling at prices less than "cash per share," in other words, less than the cash a company had in the bank divided by the number of shares in the company, even though these same companies may have had other assets amounting to four or five times the cost of the stocks. Thus, a company with one million shares outstanding may have been selling at $1 per share, even though it had $2 million in cash in the bank, $8 million in assets and no debts. If liquidated, the company would have produced $2 a share in cash and $8 a share in other assets.

At this time, from another perspective, one saw stocks selling at one-half, one-third or even one-fifth of "book value." Book value is the total assets of the company, minus all its debts, divided by the total number of shares of stock. In other words, the amount remaining if the company were to sell everything, pay its debts and distribute the difference among its shareholders. When the market is high, stocks typically sell at or above their book values.

The Cycle of Highs and Lows

When do stockbrokers do most of their business? When times are good, when the market has been rising for one or two years, when customers come in because they've heard how well their friends are doing. The higher the stock market goes, the more enthusiasm is generated. People stop buying for the basic value of each share; they buy because a friend has made money in the market. By way of illustration, look at Figure 4.1. Point A represents a market peak. People were paying very high multipliers for stocks. Point B represents a period of doom and gloom. No one would buy a stock, no matter how low the price.

In the late 1960s, when the stock market was going up, people were so anxious to buy stocks in some companies that there were numerous examples of stocks selling at between 40 and 60 times earnings, even in the case of companies which had no growth history and/or management experience—only a fancy name. If the words "computer," "nuclear," "advanced" or "technology" were part of the name of a company, they could have tremendous impact on the price of a stock.

This was a period when people were hungry to play the game. Sooner or later, however, the bubble always bursts. A piece of bad economic news may receive a lot of attention in the press, there may suddenly be discussion about stocks being overpriced, people take their money out of the markets and the cycle reverses itself: Selling begets selling.

Another Market Indicator—Dividend Yields

Another useful tool, in addition to looking at the P/E ratios of the stock market, is to look at the dividend yields in the market. Figure 4.3 shows the dividend yields of the Standard & Poor's 500 from 1961 to mid-1987. The higher the average yield (a ratio of dividend over purchase price) of stocks, the safer the time is to buy stocks. All other things being equal, you'd rather buy stocks that yield five percent than those paying you dividends that yield a three percent return on the purchase price. In looking at the graph in Figure 4.3, this very commonsense way of looking at value is a fairly effective tool historically. You see a peak in 1974 at 4.7 percent (Point A). This was the end of the 1973–74 bear market, a time when stocks were bargains and a great time to buy. Before the dramatic run in stocks from 1982 to 1987 the Standard & Poor's yield hit a high of 5.7 percent (Point B). The chart does not bode well for those buying stocks in mid-1987, as the yields of the Standard & Poor's 500 are reaching a historical low.

Swimming Against the Tide

Success in the stock market is determined to a great extent by strength of conviction. When everybody's winning, the game seems very exciting; when everybody's losing, it can feel dismal and foreboding. Common sense and basic knowledge will lead you to conclude that the depressed cycle might, in fact, be the very time to buy, but you're likely to feel lonely in your conclusion.

Aren't you at least in the company of professional money managers? Don't they buy at the bottom? No, largely because during a down cycle their customers aren't buying mutual funds and thereby supplying them with the money they need to buy stocks. As the markets improve and more people buy stocks and mutual funds, the professional money managers can add fuel to the fire.

**FIGURE 4.1   The Standard & Poor's 500 Common Stock Price
Index 1965–1975**

150 Dollars

100

A

50

B

0

1965   1970   1975

Reprinted by permission of Standard & Poor's Corp.

The important facts to remember are these. The lower the
price-earnings ratio or the multiplier is, the safer a stock is as
an investment. The higher the price-earnings ratio is, the
greater your risk will be.

What happens if you choose a stock wisely and at a time
when the market is low, only to find that the market continues
to slide? Under those circumstances, you're unlikely to do well;
due to the magnet effect of common stocks, even low risk stock
with a promising future cannot rise above a prolonged depression. However, you'll still be ahead of the pack: A low multiplier stock shouldn't go down as much as the stock market
does, even if your timing is unfortunate. Also, if the market
does go up for a couple of years, a stock that you've chosen

**FIGURE 4.2   The Standard & Poor's 500 Common Stock Price
Index 1975–1987***

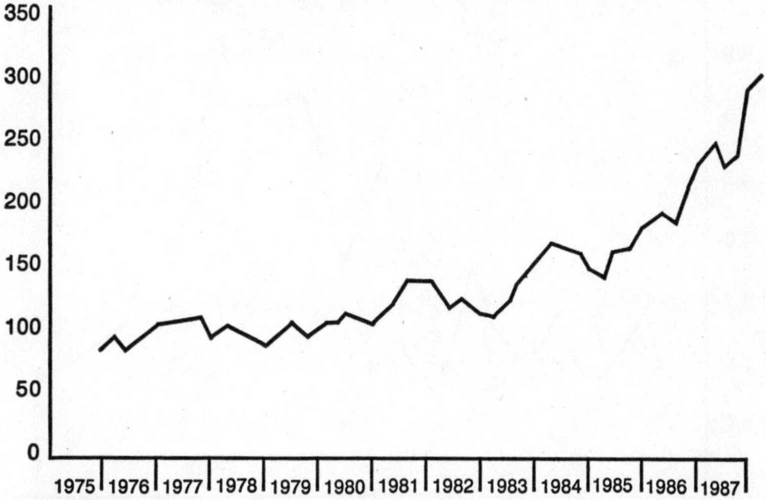

*Second quarter 1987

Reprinted by permission of Standard & Poor's Corp.

carefully should rise at a much higher rate than the market as a
whole.

The common stock price index in Figure 4.2 takes us
through mid-1987 and shows us the very good fortune of those
willing to go against the tide during the doom and gloom of
1973–74. In mid-1987, the market was pushing new highs;
these stocks were nearing 20 times earnings and were selling at
or above book value. Past experience would indicate that these
high multipliers signalled that mid-1987 was a good time to reduce one's investment in stocks.

The Crash of 1987

On October 19, 1987, investment history was made. America
experienced "Black Monday" when the Dow Jones Industrial

FIGURE 4.3   Dividend Yields of Standard & Poor's Composite 500
              Stocks 1961–1987*

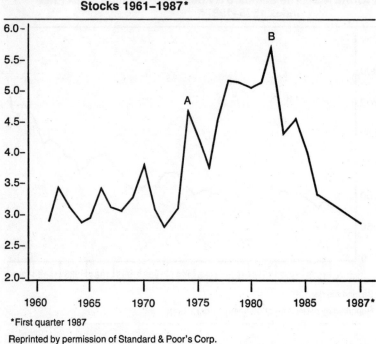

*First quarter 1987

Reprinted by permission of Standard & Poor's Corp.

Average fell 508 points—23 percent—for a $500 billion loss in one day.

Could the methods I describe in this book have helped you escape losses in the crash and avoid such a catastrophe in the future? The answer is clearly yes. If you look at Figure 4.3 above showing dividend yields, you will see that in recent history the stock market was never more overpriced. The concepts presented in Chapter 16 which compare returns on stocks, bonds and real estate, again make it clear that stocks were the most overpriced of the three. These simple formulas showed that stocks were the wrong place to have your money.

While these methods proved quite effective, they could never have predicted the swiftness of the market crash. The 23 percent drop in stock values on Black Monday was unprecedented—even in 1929 stocks only fell 12 percent in value in one day. Keep in mind, however, that part of that quick fall may have been due to today's higher level of technology which enabled so many shares of stock to trade in one day. Without such technology, stocks might have fallen just as much, but would have taken longer to do it. Even after the stocks fell to that value, historically stocks were still selling above the average price-earnings ratio and below the average dividend yield of the past 25 years. In other words, even after the crash, stocks were not cheap, but, by the standards and measures described in this book, merely reasonable.

While writing this book, it became clear to me that it was time to get out of the market, and I reviewed all my individual stocks. While the market was highly overpriced, my individual stocks stood up under analysis. Each one was at a reasonable price-to-sales ratio and price-earnings ratio; each seemed to be a good investment. What I learned was that, even if I pick the right stocks, if the market is way out of line, the right stocks go down along with the overpriced stocks when the market readjusts. I lost almost as much, percentage-wise, as others did even though I picked excellent values. As Ken Fisher stated in his *Forbes* column after the crash, the lesson he learned from the Crash of 1987 was that if a freight train is coming, get off the tracks.

The added lesson that I haven't included in detail in this book is *discipline*. In a period of euphoria, there are always rational explanations why stocks will go even higher. This time people said yes, stocks are high, but they'll go higher because the Japanese market is so much more overpriced than ours that money will come into our stock market from Japan. Or, they said that earnings are going to grow a great deal during 1988 and today's high multipliers will seem justified by then. There are always plausible-sounding explanations for why one shouldn't sell when stocks are overpriced. There is always an expert who will say that stocks are going to go even higher. You must have the discipline to stick with your guidelines.

Finally, at some level I was less wary than I should have been because so many investment advisors and so much of the financial press were talking about the coming collapse in stock prices. Typically crashes come as a surprise, when almost everyone is optimistic. As a contrarian, I always assume it's a good sign if everyone thinks the market is going to crash and a bad sign if everyone thinks the market is going to go up. This has taught me not to go against what people think or with what people think, but first and foremost to look at value.

Let me repeat this essential point. Don't get caught up in the euphoria or the doom and gloom that may surround you. Know your rules, trust them and trust yourself.

Like the wise man says, to thine own self be true. To do well, you must continually monitor your own compass, use your own instincts, trust your gut and above all, use common sense.

5

The Mechanics of Common Stocks

Without the basics, you're in a canoe without a paddle.

This chapter is full of things that you have to know in order to operate in the stock market. Since some of it is detailed and involves the mechanical aspects of investing, I'd suggest that you eat a hot-fudge sundae, burn some incense or do something else to help you relax while you burrow through this information. Without the basics, you're in a canoe without a paddle.

Stock Splits

When a company gives you one or more shares of stock for every share you now own, it's called a *stock split*. For example, let's say Company X has one million shares of stock outstanding. For each of these shares, Company X sends its stockholders a second share, so that by the time the company is through mailing out all this stock, there are two million shares outstanding. If before the stock split you owned 100 shares of stock in the company, you would now own 200. However, you really haven't improved your lot, because you still own the same *percentage* of the company as you did before. The company has twice as many shares outstanding, so each share you have is worth one-half as much as it was before—as the market price will reflect. You may have twice as many shares, but essentially you've gotten nowhere. However, there's a method to the company's madness.

By splitting the stock (if the split's two-for-one), the price of the stock is likely to go down by one-half. This means that if the stock was selling at $40 a share, it will probably now be selling at $20. As a result, over time the company is likely to get a wider participation of ownership in the company, because if the stock is selling at a lower price, more people can afford to buy shares. If it's a company that sells a lot of goods to consumers, it may feel that it is going to get more consumer loyalty by having a larger number of shareholders. For example, if you happen to own stock in General Electric (G. E.) and are shopping for an electric toaster, you might pick one made by G. E. because you're a shareholder in the company.

How would the company get all these new shares? It's simple. It would just print them with the approval of its board of directors. So, if you find out that the company in which you own stock is going to have a stock split, you can feel okay about it, but don't get too excited—it's usually not a very material bit of news, although it might cause a little enthusiasm among investors and the stock may go up a point or two.

It is good news, however, if the company splitting the stock also has an overall dividend increase. For example, if the stock had been paying a $1 dividend and splits two-for-one, then it would be paying 50 cents a share on the new shares and your total dividend would be the same. However, if the company leaves the dividend the same and splits two-for-one, then the dividend doubles. More common is a situation wherein the company rises the dividend only slightly. For example, if the dividend was $1, and after the split is 60 cents, you're now getting $1.20 on your two shares instead of $1 on your one old share. This may cause the price to go up somewhat.

Stock Dividends

A *stock dividend* is really a ministock split: A stock split of less than one share for one. For example, a company may distribute one share to you for every 20 you now own. In essence it's a fractional stock split. The company may give you ten percent of the number of shares you already own, or five percent, or 20 percent or 50 percent. Some companies give stock dividends in lieu of cash dividends every year. Some people invariably regard these stock dividends in the same way they would cash dividends.

If you own 100 shares and the company pays a ten percent stock dividend, you'll own 110 shares—but you'll still have the same interest in the company as before the dividend. In other words, your 110 shares represent ownership of the same percentage of that company as did your initial 100 shares. A company doesn't have to make any profits to pay a stock dividend; all it has to do is print certificates and mail them to you. If you look at these as dividends and sell them on the market every time you get them, you'll just be reducing your ownership in the company and not really collecting profits of the company.

Margin

Stockbrokers will lend you money to buy stock. At the present time they will lend 50 percent of the price of a stock if you put up the other 50 percent. That is called buying on *margin*. (This percentage varies with government regulations. Before the 1929 crash you could borrow 90 percent of the price.) If you buy 100 shares of stock for $100 a share, that is $10,000 worth of stock. If you're buying on margin, you put up only $5,000 in cash and the stockbroker lends you the other $5,000. However, he'll charge you an interest rate a little bit above the prime rate that the big corporations have to pay. This rate has varied in the past 20 years from a low of five percent to a high of 22 percent.

The basic effect of buying (or borrowing) on margin is to amplify both your gains and your losses. Let's say you have $5,000 in cash to invest in a stock and it's selling at $50 a share. You have a choice: You can either buy 100 shares at $50 a share for $5,000, or you can ask your stockbroker to lend you $5,000 and buy 200 shares. You'd be spending $10,000, half of which doesn't belong to you.

If you buy the stock for $5,000 cash and the stock doubles in price, going from $50 to $100 a share, then you sell and make a $5,000 profit. However, if the stock drops in value by 50 percent to a price of $25 a share and then you sell, you are going to lose $2,500. Table 5.1 shows what happens if you buy on margin.

If the stock doubles and goes from $50 to $100 a share, you've done much better than you would using your cash alone. After one year you can sell the stock for $20,000, paying back the broker the $5,000 you borrowed, which leaves you with $15,000, or a profit of $10,000. Thus, while the stock only doubled, you tripled your money.

However, if the stock had gone down by 50 percent, your 200 shares would be worth only $5,000. Consequently, after you paid the stockbroker back the $5,000 you borrowed, you'd be left with nothing, having lost $5,000. So, using margin, you can increase your gains or you can increase your losses. If your crystal ball is working well and you know a stock is going to go up, you're better off buying on margin. Keep in mind, however, *you're taking bigger risks.* Also, don't forget the interest cost, which we didn't compute in this example. You pay interest on that borrowed money, so your profit actually would have been a little less than $10,000 in the first example and your loss would have been a little greater than $5,000 in the second example.

TABLE 5.1   Buying on Margin

Assume an investor buys $10,000 worth of stock: $5,000 cash and $5,000 borrowed from stockbroker.

200 shares at $50 a share	$10,000 (market value)
Less loan due stockbroker	5,000
Net equity or value	$5,000

Changes in net equity after one year:

	Stock remains at $50	Stock doubles to $100	Stock declines to $25
Market value of stock	$10,000	$20,000	$5,000
Less loan due stockbroker	5,000	5,000	5,000
Net equity	$5,000	$15,000	$ 0

Margin is not a wise tool for most small investors to use. Even when you've made a correct judgment on a long-term basis, a stock might initially go down as much as 20 percent, 30 percent or even 40 percent. As the stock goes down, the broker will call you and insist that you put up more cash as security. If you can't or don't want to, he or she will sell your stock. After all, the broker treats the stock as collateral, so as its value goes down, he or she wants more cash. This means you might be forced to sell at a loss a stock, which, in the long run, you were correct in buying. For example, you may have bought a stock at $50 that you were forced to sell when it went down to $30 and which subsequently went up to $150. In my experience this is not uncommon. If a stock is worth a lot more than its selling price, for whatever reasons, the stock may go even lower a month or two after buying it, but then will go considerably higher in six months to one or two years. In these cases, if I had bought on margin and didn't have any more cash to back me up, I might have been forced out of a position that could have otherwise been profitable. So unless you have a rich aunt or uncle from whom you can draw cash if you need it, buying on margin adds an element of gamble to investing. You're gambling that the stock will go up immediately and I don't know anyone who can predict successfully the day-to-day movements of a stock.

Selling Short

Selling short means selling shares you don't own. You're betting that the stock will go down. Here's how it works.

Your friend thinks stock in Fat Farms, Inc. is hot. You tell your friend he or she is wrong. The stock is selling at $100 a share. You offer to sell your friend a share at $100. Your friend hands you $100. You say, "Give me ten days and I'll hand you the stock." Your friend says, "Fine." Ten days later the stock is trading at $60. You peel off six of those bills your friend gave you and buy a share. You give your friend the stock you owed he or her and keep the four other bills.

Well, that's the idea—but here's how it really works. You go to your stockbroker and say, "I think that stock ABO is going down. It's at $10 a share right now. So I want to sell 100 shares short." Your broker puts in an order to sell as if you owned the stock. Somebody buys that stock for $10 a share and, of course, the purchaser wants his or her stock, having paid a total of $1,000 for it. So your broker finds a client who happens to own 100 shares of ABO Corporation and says to that client, "Look, you don't have any plans to buy or sell any more of that stock; it's just sitting in your vault. Would you mind loaning it to us? We'll pay you an interest rate for the use of your stock and you can keep collecting your dividends." (As a "short seller," you would have to pay the interest and the dividends.)

Since the person who is holding that stock in a vault doesn't have anything to lose by lending it to the broker, he or she does so. The broker gives this stock to the buyer and holds the $1,000 received from the buyer in trust. So the person you really owe the stock to isn't the person who just bought it; you owe the stock to the broker, who in turn owes it to that friendly customer who had it sitting in a vault. The security you're going to use to pay the broker for the stock you sold short is $1,000 (the price of the stock), so that he or she knows you had the purchasing power to buy the stock.

If all goes well and the stock goes down to $3, you then ask the broker to buy the stock. The broker uses part of your $1,000 to buy the stock and returns the 100 shares to the original person who lent it to the broker. Then the broker gives you your $700, plus the other $1,000 received from the buyer of the stock in the original transaction. Remember, when you sold that stock short you gave the broker $1,000 to hold. But the buyer of that stock also paid for it, and that money also wound up in your broker's hands.

Look at this another way. Let's say that the stock you sold short at $10 started to rise instead of fall and that within three months it is priced at $20. The broker is sitting with $2,000 in trust ($1,000 from you and $1,000 from the buyer). Now the cost of buying 100 shares is $2,000. The broker will get you on the phone and say, "Look, if you don't come up with more cash for us to hold in trust, we're going to have to buy this stock right now." If the broker does go out and buy it, and it takes all of the $2,000 to buy these shares on the market and to deliver them back to the person who had them in the vault, then you're out your full investment of $1,000.

Of course, things could get worse. If the stock triples, you're not only out of your original $1,000—your whole investment—but you also owe the broker additional money. If the stock goes to $30, you will lose $2,000. If the stock goes to $100, you might lose $9,000. When you sell short, there's no limit to how much you can lose. There is, however, a limit to how much you can make. At best you can double your money. If the stock went from $10 to $0 you wouldn't have to buy the stock at all and that $2,000 trust fund your broker is holding all goes to you. Your $1,000 would have turned into $2,000. Therefore, be careful and always keep in mind you can only double your money when you sell short, but you can lose an infinite amount.

Options—Puts and Calls

Calls. A *call* is the right to buy 100 shares of stock at a specific price for a specific period of time. For example, someone may sell you the right to buy 100 shares of American Telephone and Telegraph at a price of $56 a share anytime between today and six months from today. The stock may be selling now at $56 a share. In three months, if the stock is at $70 a share, you still would have the right to buy the stock at $56. Your $300 (the price of the call) would have been well spent, because if a stock is selling at $70 but you have the right to buy it at $56, you can buy at $56 and immediately sell it at $70. In other words, you've got the opportunity to make $1,400 less the $300 you paid to buy the call, or a net profit of $1,100.

If you think a stock is going to go up *in the very near future* and you want to maximize your gains, then the call is the best and most efficient way to do it.

Let's say you have $1,000 to invest and you believe stock ABO, now selling at $10 per share, is going to double to $20 a share during the next six months. You know that if you invest your $1,000 in the stock, you can buy 100 shares at $10 each. Six months later, when the stock reaches $20, you can sell it for $2,000. In other words, you will double your money. However, let's see what happens if you invest your $1,000 in calls on this stock, rather than buying it outright. Let's say that you can buy a call (the right to buy 100 shares) of ABO Corporation for $100. The call extends for six months; i.e., for six months you have the right to buy 100 shares of ABO at $10 each. Thereafter you have no rights regarding the stock. You can buy ten calls with your $1,000. Remember, each call gives you the right to buy 100 shares, so you now have the right to buy a total of 1,000 shares at $10 each. If ABO did move from $10 to $20 within six months, you would have made much more than you would have by just buying the stock.

Suppose you could borrow the money to buy 1,000 shares at $10, exercise your option (buy the stock) and then sell the 1,000 shares immediately at $20. You make $10 a share—or

$10,000—less the $1,000 you invested in the calls. Your profit is $9,000 versus the $1,000 you would have made by buying the stock outright. (In reality, you would simply sell the calls for $10,000 and not have to go through the bother of buying and selling the stock.) Calls rise in value along with the rise in value of the stock.

From this synopsis it may seem as if you should always buy calls rather than just buying stock. However, there are a lot of different risks in buying calls. If, for example, the stock had stayed at $10 a share and didn't go either up or down, after six months your right to buy the stock at $10 would have expired; all calls have a time limit. Obviously, there would have been no sense in exercising the calls and buying the stock at $10. The calls, therefore, would become worthless at the end of the six-month period, and you would lose the entire $1,000 investment, even though the stock didn't go down. Had you bought the stock for $1,000 (i.e., $10 a share), you wouldn't have lost anything—you would have broken even. Therefore, though you stand a chance of making a lot of money with a call, you also stand a chance of losing more money.

When you buy a call, you not only have to be right that a stock is undervalued and will go up; you also have to have good timing—it has to go up in a short period of time. *The vast majority of calls are never exercised.* In other words, most people never buy the stock and just let the call expire, thereby losing their investment. On the other hand, if you are successful, as we saw in the example, you can do exceptionally well. It's a gamble.

Puts. A *put* is the reverse of a call. It's the right to sell 100 shares of stock at a specified price for a specified period of time. A put is a way of betting that a stock is going to go down and that it will do this in a very short time span.

For example, if you believe that ABO Corporation stock, now at $10 a share, is going to go down to $5 a share, and you have $1,000 to invest, you might want to buy ten puts for $100 each, giving you the right to sell this stock at $10 a share for the next six months. If your prediction is right, and the stock does go down to $5 a share, you'll be glad to sell this stock to someone at $10 per share. Of course, you don't own the stock. You have to find someone who will give you $10 a share so that you can go out and buy the stock at $5 and deliver it to him or her. You might be wondering, "Who's going to give me $10 a share for stock selling at $5?" Well, the person who sold you the put is under an obligation to give you $10 a share.

This means, then, that if the stock goes down to $5, you make a $5,000 profit, less the cost of the puts, or a $4,000 net profit. If the stock stays at the same price or goes up, however, you lose all your money. Keep in mind that the alternative to betting the stock is going to go down through buying puts, is to sell short. You could take your $1,000 and sell 100 shares short. If the stock goes down to $5, you will then make a profit of $500.

Buying a put is a viable alternative to selling short. Remember—when you sell short you can lose an infinite amount of money. If you sell the ABO Corporation stock at $10 and it goes up to $20, you will lose all your investment; if it goes up to $30 you will lose all your investment plus another 100 percent of your investment, and so on. Again, buying a put means that you're betting the stock is going to go down. If you're right, you're going to make money; if you're wrong, you can lose only what you paid for the put. Your loss, therefore, is limited. Therefore, if you really believe a stock is going to go down and you believe it is going to happen very quickly, not only will you make more money by buying puts rather than selling short, you might also sleep better. On the other hand, if the stock winds up neither going down nor going up, you would have been better off selling short, because you would have broken even.

Index Options. An *index option* is a call for a put on a cross section of stocks. If you have a strong hunch or a certain vision of a sharp move in the stock market, but are not up to researching individual companies, index options will fill the bill.

Several such options are available, but the most frequently used is the S & P 100 Index Options. The S & P 100 are 100 large corporations that have puts and calls traded on the Chicago Board Options Exchange. As the aggregate price of the stocks moves up and down, the index follows suit (like the Dow Jones averages).

For a specific premium you can buy the right to control 100 times the index in cash. Let us say the index is 150 and you buy a three-month call giving you the right to "buy the index" at 150. You then have $150 × 100, or $15,000, in play. If during those three months the market soars 15 percent your index will trade at $172.50. Your gain would be $172.50 × 100 ($17,250) less $15,000, or $2,250. From that profit you must subtract the cost or premium paid for this option. That cost would have been approximately $600, so your net profit would be $1,650.

Again, if the market had remained the same or if it had gone down, your investment of $600 would have been worth nothing.

Similar index options include Value Line Index Options, NYSE Index Options, American Stock Exchange Options and the S & P 500 Index.

I do not see index options as a useful tool for most investors because they are not like buying a mutual fund: If you're not correct right away (three to six months) you lose everything. Index options are for gamblers, speculators or professional traders.

Puts and calls are good investments only when stocks move dramatically and quickly and when you've done your homework carefully.

Warrants

Warrants are similar to calls, except that they are instruments put out directly by the corporation itself. To raise extra capital a corporation may sell to the public the right to buy its stock at a certain price and for a certain period of time, usually a very long period of time. For example, XYZ Corporation may sell to the public the right to buy 100 shares of its stock at $10 a share any time in the next 12 years. The stock presently may be selling at $3 a share, so that right doesn't seem valuable. Furthermore, the company may sell the right for the equivalent of 50 cents a share. In other words, for $50 (100 shares at 50 cents a share) the company may sell the right for you to buy 100 shares of stock in this company any time in the next 12 years at a price of $10 a share. Warrants have one big advantage over buying a call—you have a lot of time for the stock to do what you hope it's going to do. When you buy a call you might be right about the future of the company and you might be right that the stock is undervalued, but the rise in price might not occur in the short time period in which your call exists. If you buy a warrant with a substantial length of time and if you're right about the present value of the stock, the market price will go up and this investment will become profitable before your warrant expires.

6

Mutual Funds

Mutual funds offer diversification, that is, an opportunity to invest in 20 or 30 different companies rather than in two or three, and they also offer professional management.

In the early 1960s the stock market looked like a good place to invest money. If you had invested anytime between 1928 and 1965, randomly selecting stocks, you could have made a nine percent return on your money if you had let the investment just sit. This doesn't mean that you couldn't have lost money by picking the wrong stocks. Some stocks went down in value, or went up very little. On the average, however, your *capital growth*—that is, price appreciation and dividends—would have equalled a compound return of about nine percent on your money. In that era of low interest rates and five percent passbook accounts, that was very impressive.

In 1965 a lot of people wanted to invest in the stock market because it had been such a successful investment for others. Many knew little about choosing stocks, felt uncomfortable buying stocks themselves and didn't have enough money to buy a large selection of stocks. Along came the phenomenon of *mutual funds*, which solved these problems for small inves-

FIGURE 6.1   Assets of Stock Mutual Funds 1961–1987*

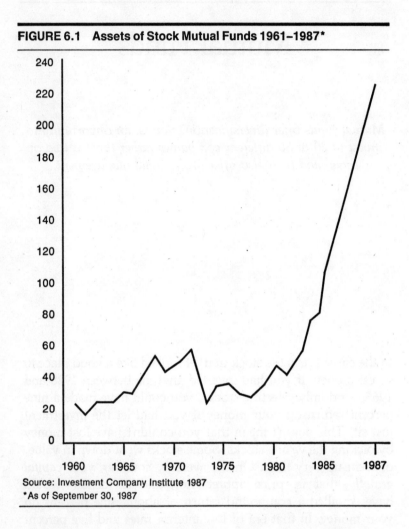

Source: Investment Company Institute 1987
*As of September 30, 1987

tors. Since that embryonic period, their growth has been phe-
nomenal.

The mutual fund phenomenon worked this way. A person
would set up a service for the small investor. This person
would say to the investor, "I'm going to go out and buy $1 mil-
lion worth of stocks and put them all into one fund. I'll buy

what I consider to be 30 or 40 of the leading stocks with the best prospects. If you give me $1,000 you can own part of this fund, along with other investors, each of whom will also spend $1,000 for a share. I will sell 1,000 shares at $1,000 each and that's where the total of $1 million comes from. Each of you will own a proportionate share of the total fund. If at any time in the future you want to sell your share, you can, and you'll receive its market value." If the operator of the mutual fund went out and invested the $1 million in stocks and two years later the stocks were worth $1.2 million, then the stocks increased in value 20 percent. If you wanted to sell your share in this mutual fund, you'd get $1,200 for your $1,000 investment (a 20 percent increase). Since the value of the fund went up 20 percent, your share would go up 20 percent. Mutual funds offer diversification, that is, an opportunity to invest in 20 or 30 different companies rather than in two or three, and they also offer professional management—people who are experts in selecting stocks that are going to do better than average. The hope is that if the stock market goes up, you'll do even better than the market averages with mutual funds.

But there are costs to the mutual fund investor. Many mutual funds have a *load fee* that may run as high as eight percent. This means that if you pay $1,000 to buy an interest in mutual funds, about eight percent of that would be used as commissions, partly for your stockbroker and partly for the mutual fund manager. So actually, you get $920 worth of stock in a mutual fund for your $1,000 investment ($1,000 minus $80 commission). You are immediately *down* eight percent, which means that the mutual fund's stocks (portfolio) will have to rise by more than eight percent before you'll break even.

Operators of mutual funds often do quite well financially. They make their money by setting up a company to manage the mutual fund and then directing the fund to use this management company's services. The management company charges anywhere from .25 percent to one percent a year of the total amount of money managed. In other words, if a mutual fund has $10 million invested in it, the management company might get one percent or $100,000 a year for deciding which stocks to buy and sell.

If you were running a management company that managed a mutual fund, your strongest motivation would be for that mutual fund to grow, because the more money you manage, the higher the fees you'll collect. How can you continue selling more shares in a mutual fund? Look at the first example. Once you've sold the 1,000 shares at $1,000 each, how can you raise more money? The answer is this: You can expand if you have an *open-end mutual fund,* which is the most typical type of mutual fund. All you have to do is find out what one share in the mutual fund is worth and offer more shares to the public at that value.

Again, let's say the fund has 1,000 shares and the total fund is worth $1 million. Therefore, each share in that fund is worth $1,000. In an open-end mutual fund anyone who wants to can put up $1,000 and will be issued another share. This doesn't dilute the ownership of the initial 1,000 investors; even if the whole fund were to be doubled by selling another 1,000 shares at $1,000 each, all the shares are still worth $1,000. Similarly, if the fund had gone from $1 million to $1.2 million in market value, these new shares would be sold for $1,200 each, and this too wouldn't hurt the interests of the previous owners. There's one problem, however. The bigger your fund becomes, the more difficult it is to manage successfully and to make a lot of money for its shareholders.

When a mutual fund becomes so large that it's managing, let's say, $1 billion, it's not worthwhile for the fund to bother buying shares in promising small companies because by investing even $100,000 or $200,000 in a company, the mutual fund might drive the price of that stock up by as much as 50 percent or even 100 percent. Also, even if you find a small company with stock selling at, let's say, $4 a share and a total of 500,000 shares outstanding, if you bought all the stock in that company and somehow did this without driving the market price up, that would involve only $2 million, an insignificant amount in comparison with the $1 billion you're managing. Therefore, even if you did pick a winner and you could buy all that stock, you still would have very little effect on the total outcome of the fund.

As mutual funds become larger, they have to move into markets that deal in huge, mature corporations. Unlike you and me, they can't just buy 200 or 300 shares of the stock and hope it goes up. That's insignificant. They have to buy 10,000, 20,000 or 40,000 shares of stock at a time. With some exceptions, the bulk of their activity is on the New York Stock Exchange. For reasons we discussed earlier, there aren't many stocks on the New York Stock Exchange that are likely to do spectacularly well, mainly because by the time they are listed there they are past their stage of rapid growth.

You might be wondering why buying large numbers of shares in small companies will drive up the price of a stock. It's a simple law of supply and demand. You have to find people to sell stock if you're going to buy it. If a stock's bid price is $4 and the asking price is $4.50 you will buy some at $4.50. Fairly soon you'll have exhausted all people who are willing to sell at $4.50. In order to buy more stock, you'll have to find people who are willing to sell at $4.75 or $5; as these are exhausted, the price will keep moving up. So the greater the buying pressure, the more you have to pay to buy stock. The smaller the company, the fewer the dollars needed for this phenomenon to occur.

The fact that managers of mutual funds, pension funds and trust funds often can't invest successfully in the very small over-the-counter companies can be to your benefit because when you're investing in small, promising companies, you will have less competition. There's a greater chance of finding an underpriced stock that's been ignored by the professionals. The smaller the companies are that you look at, the less likely it is you're going to be competing with professional investors.

All of this means that a smaller mutual fund has greater potential for big gains than does a huge fund. Therefore, try to find the small fund with a good track record.

Mutual funds, over time, don't seem to do any better as a group than randomly selected stocks. While from year to year some funds do better than others, *on average, investing your money in mutual funds is no better than throwing darts at a newspaper and picking the stocks where the darts may fall.* As a matter of fact, you'd probably do a little better throwing the darts. The main reason for this is the load fee (the eight percent you may pay to get into the fund), which puts you a year behind before you start.

Besides selecting smaller mutual funds instead of the larger ones, you can do one other very helpful thing.

Winning in the Mutual Fund Game: No-Load Funds

In addition to hundreds of "load" mutual funds, there are hundreds of "low-load" and "no-load" mutual funds. These have fees of zero percent to two percent or three percent. According to the Investment Company Institute, of 2,300 total mutual funds as of mid-1987, 53 percent were load funds and 47 percent were no-load funds. If you buy shares in a no-load fund, you start out even instead of down eight percent. You do gain diversification—i.e., your $1,000 is spread over 30 to 50 companies' stocks rather than the two or three you might have bought on your own.

Surprisingly, no-load funds perform as well as load funds. Why, then, do people buy load funds? While hosting a radio program on investments, I put that questions to the director of a firm selling millions of dollars of load funds. I asked how he could justify this charge. His answer was that while the no-load funds on average performed as well as load funds, the load fee is earned by the salesperson (broker) in steering you into a mutual fund. In other words, you earn less because you are paying someone to hold your hand. In recent years, many investment management companies have organized families of mutual funds. Such families consist of from two to over 20 mutual funds with different investment policies. The benefit of investing in a no-load mutual fund that is a member of a family of funds is that the shareholder can switch from one fund to another without charge. Such switches are effected by a single telephone call followed by a small amount of paperwork after the transaction has taken place. Thus, investors can alter their investment portfolios with relative ease whenever their objectives or their assessments of the investment climate change. This is still a sale-purchase situation, merely facilitated by the telephoning. Therefore, except for retirement plans such as Keoghs, *capital gains taxes will be assessed accordingly.*

There are numerous newsletters and books devoted to mutual funds. I would recommend a look at *The Individual Investor's Guide to No-Load Mutual Funds* by Gerald W. Peritt & L. Kay Shannon.

7

Inflation and the Stock Market

Inflation is not, in and of itself, a danger to investing in the stock market; in fact, stocks can be an excellent inflation hedge.

Most investment counselors and people who write about investments agree that inflation is bad for the stock market; that is, inflation results in lower stock prices instead of higher stock prices. The logic is: If there is an eight percent rate of inflation, you're going to demand a higher rate of return on stocks than if there were no inflation at all. After all, you're losing eight percent in purchasing power every year on those dollars that are invested in the stock, so if the stock goes up only eight percent in price and pays no dividend, you're not making money. You're getting eight percent more dollars, but the dollars buy eight percent less. In other words, if you buy a stock at $100 a share and in a year it's worth $108, you can't buy any more this year with the $108 than you could last year with the $100.

If that stock selling for $100 is selling at ten times earnings and people become concerned about inflation, they'll pay a lower multiplier. They'll say, "Why should I pay ten times earnings to get a ten percent rate of return when there's so much inflation? I want at least a 12.5 percent rate of return." Consequently, the multiplier would drop to eight times earnings. If you pay $80 for a stock that's earning $10, you're making a 12.5 percent rate of return. Therefore, the higher the rate of inflation, the lower the multipliers will be that people will attach to stocks when they determine what the stocks are worth.

In the great recession of 1974, when stocks had their biggest fall since the Depression, people had to adjust to double-digit inflation. Most people saw double-digit inflation becoming a permanent part of American life and they began to demand much higher rates of return from their investments. People who wanted to borrow money had to pay a much higher interest rate to get that money. Since people had alternative ways of using their money other than buying stock, they also demanded a higher rate of return on their stocks, because they could get a higher rate of return by lending their money to the government or to corporations via bonds. While in 1967 people were willing to pay 14 or 15 times earnings, in 1974 they would pay only five or six times earnings because they wanted compensation for the erosion of their purchasing power. However, playing the market and taking inflation into account at the same time is very complicated. The following simplifies that process, makes it comprehensible, and explains my theory of inflation and the stock market.

Whether or not there is inflation isn't significant in figuring out the future of stock prices in general. What is important is the *change* in the rate of inflation. As the rate of inflation subsides, multipliers increase. People are willing to pay a more generous multiplier for the same earnings from a corporation as inflation subsides. We saw this in 1976: As inflation went from a rate of 12 percent to a rate of about six percent, people were more willing to pay ten times earnings for stocks, instead of six times earnings, because they didn't see their purchasing power eroding as rapidly. We saw it again in 1981 through 1987 as the Reagan administration brought the inflation rate down and stocks soared in response. One of the reasons that 1974 was a good time to buy stocks was that when the rate of inflation was at 12 percent, multipliers had adjusted to this rate of inflation. When people were paying three, four or five times earnings, they were paying a very low price for the present earnings of corporations. If the rate of inflation had stayed at 12 percent—a horrendous rate of inflation—stocks wouldn't have gone much lower, because the multipliers had already adjusted to it and would have stayed the same. If earnings had continued to grow, the price of stocks would have increased as well. There was, of course, the risk that inflation would get worse. If it had, multipliers would probably have gone even lower, although they really couldn't go much lower.

For a broad perspective, look at Figure 7.1. You'll see that low inflation from 1960 to 1973 kept multipliers high. Conversely, as inflation increased in the 1974–1984 period, multipliers fell dramatically, hitting levels not seen since 1951.

Inflation is not, in and of itself, a danger to investing in the stock market; in fact, stocks can be an excellent inflation hedge. It's a bad investment if, and only if, people haven't already taken into account how inflation will affect their investment decisions. When the market slid in 1974 people began to adjust to inflation. Today, people are paying a multiplier based on the present rate of inflation. If inflation stays at its present rate and doesn't get any worse, then it should not affect multipliers adversely. On the other hand, if the rate of inflation goes down, people will pay higher and higher multipliers for the earnings of stocks. It's good to be in the stock market when inflation is high; it's not good to be in the stock market when the rate of inflation is low, but is on the verge of accelerating.

In a way, if there is inflation, then the stock market is a good place for your money. Let's hypothesize that for the next ten years we have an inflation rate of six percent a year. If multipliers have already adjusted to that rate of inflation—in other words, if people are paying multipliers low enough to give them rates of return that will compensate them for their losses

---

**FIGURE 7.1   Average Market Price-Earnings Ratios and Inflation
1950–August 1987**

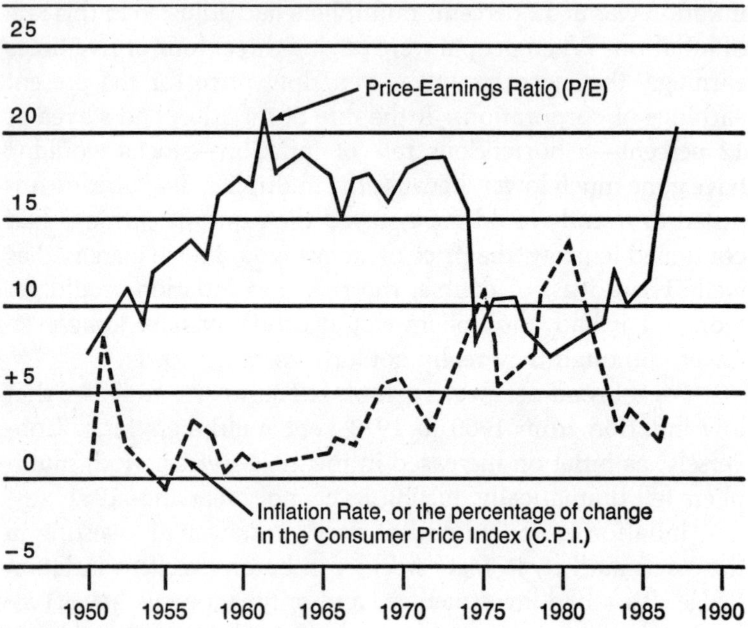

Price-Earnings Ratio (P/E)

Inflation Rate, or the percentage of change in the Consumer Price Index (C.P.I.)

1950   1955   1960   1965   1970   1975   1980   1985   1990

*Author's estimate as of this writing.

---

in purchasing power because of inflation—then stocks are a hedge against inflation. Let's say the average multiplier is nine and at that level people are satisified to own stocks if the rate of inflation stays at six percent. This means that the multiplier will stay at about nine and that earnings will likely go up by at least six percent even if companies don't grow at all, just because of inflation. Therefore, stocks are likely to go up in dollar value six percent a year. In addition, as already mentioned, companies tend to grow in real sales in a predictable pattern: first moderately, then rapidly and finally slowly. Inflation should put an automatic growth factor of about six percent into these stocks, in addition to their own volume growth of business. Thus, once the market has reached equilibrium and has accounted for the present rate of inflation, stocks will be in fact a hedge against inflation. This may sound crazy, but I really believe it's true. In the 1950s and 1960s it was common folklore that the stock market was a hedge against inflation; that is, until we had substantial double-digit inflation. Now common wisdom is that only real commodities such as real estate, art, diamonds and coins are a hedge against inflation. I don't think this is true. Even if the rate of inflation becomes extremely high in the future, once the stock market adjusts for those rates (if they don't get any worse) it would again act as a hedge. But remember: You don't want to be in the market while it is still making adjustments to accelerating inflation rates.

In conclusion, *buy when inflation is subsiding and sell when inflation is accelerating.*

8

Preferred Stocks and Bonds

A bond from Apple Computer isn't worth more in the marketplace than one from General Motors, even though Apple is currently a rapid growth company while GM's growth is slow.

Corporate Bonds

If a corporation wants to borrow money and wants to go to the public to borrow the money rather than to a bank or an insurance company, it will sell bonds. Essentially, a bond is a loan, usually issued in denominations of $1,000. If you buy a bond you're buying an IOU, for example, from General Motors, American Telephone or Standard Oil of Ohio, and the corporation pays you interest on the loan. Just as with common stocks, the first sale of the bond puts the money in the corporate treasury and from that point on the bond is traded in the securities markets between new buyers and sellers. Unlike stocks, however, bonds usually have a *maturity* date, a date at which the corporation returns the face value of the bonds. For example, IBM may issue a $1,000 bond that pays 12 percent interest a year and promise that at the end of 20 years it will pay back the $1,000. Unless IBM goes bankrupt, you won't lose your money. The corporation has no choice—it must pay you interest every year and must pay the full principal back to you at the end of 20 years. If it doesn't, you can sue the corporation for the money and it must pay or go bankrupt. There are always risks in any investment, but buying corporate bonds in large U.S. corporations is a very low-risk investment. Two services—Standard & Poor's and Moody's—give out safety ratings on corporate bonds ranging from AAA (the highest) to C. The higher the rating, the better they consider the quality of the bond.

For most investors, the main purpose for buying corporate bonds is the income. At the present time the average corporate bond gives a cash yield on an investment of about seven percent more than common stocks. The average common stock at present yields about three percent—that is, its dividends are about four percent of market price—while the average bond yields about ten percent. The other side of the coin, however, is that a bond is a lot less likely to appreciate. For this reason, people close to retirement who are looking for a high predictable income with the capital they have saved are better suited for buying bonds, whereas younger individuals trying to build up wealth and capital are better suited to investing in common stocks. Younger people who are making satisfactory incomes can afford to do without the larger interest yield, whereas older people who have retired are not trying to build up estates for use 25 years in the future, but need higher incomes in the present.

When you buy a corporate bond your primary concern should be safety. Since a bond does not give you any real equity in a company, it doesn't really matter whether the corporation that issues the bond is a growth corporation or not, so long as it's able to meet the interest and principal payments on the bond. The fact that the corporation might triple in size will not increase the value of its bonds. A bond from a high technology growth company is not necessarily worth more or less than a bond in a steady, sound, low-growth corporation. If, for example, you bought a $1,000 bond that paid $120 a year in interest (12 percent a year), and the corporation grew 100-fold in the next ten years, you would still get $120 a year, no more, no less. If the slow-growing solid company sold a bond with the same terms as the growth company, you would also be earning $120 a year on your $1,000 investment, even though the company might not grow at all.

Convertible Bonds

Sometimes a corporation will sell bonds that yield a lower than normal interest rate by offering a special feature called a *conversion privilege.* If, for example, the normal interest rate on bonds is 12 percent and the corporation would like to pay a lower interest rate, they might offer the public a nine percent bond that pays nine percent on the face value of a $1,000 loan but in addition gives the buyer the right to *convert that bond* into a certain number of shares of the corporation's common stock during the life of that bond.

Let's say that ABO Corporation issues a $1,000 bond that yields nine percent annually and is convertible into 20 shares of its stock. This means that while you're holding the bond you can send it to the corporation at any time and they will exchange it for 20 shares of their common stock. Let's also say that the stock is now selling at $40 a share. Well, you'd be foolish to convert the bond now, because you'd get 20 shares of stock worth $40—a total of only $800 in market value. The value of the conversion privilege lies in the possibility that during the lifespan of the bond, the value of the stock will go up. If the stock hits $50 a share, 20 shares will equal the face value of the bond. If a few years later, however, the stock goes up to $100 a share, you can convert your bond into 20 shares which will then be worth $2,000. Thus, convertible bonds fall somewhere between a stock and a bond. You sacrifice some income for the possibility of capital appreciation. On the other hand, your income is safe because the corporation must pay the interest; as with regular bonds, the corporation is legally bound to do it.

The popularity of convertible bonds has grown dramatically in the 1980s. Value Line puts out an excellent newsletter on convertibles, and there are several low- or no-load mutual funds of convertible bonds, including Value Line and Fidelity. These are simple ways of investing in convertibles without doing research.

Preferred Stock

A *preferred stock* is another vehicle by which a corporation borrows money from investors. As with a bond, the corporation guarantees a specific, fixed dividend, but a preferred stock doesn't have a maturity date. In other words, the corporation promises to pay indefinitely a specific annual dividend, one that does not get larger as the corporation expands.

A preferred stock is an income investment; it is not a growth investment. Unlike a corporate bond, however, a corporation may elect to miss a dividend due a preferred stockholder. If you don't get paid your dividend you cannot sue the corporation and expect to recover. However, the corporation is unlikely to miss paying your dividend unless it's in financial trouble, because it is obliged to pay dividends to preferred stockholders before paying the common stockholders. If, for example, the corporation goes through some rough times for six or seven years, it can miss paying all dividends to its preferred and common stockholders during that time. However, if the corporation gets back on its feet again, it must pay the preferred stockholders their dividends before paying common dividends. If it is a "cumulative" preferred, all the missed dividends from those six or seven years must be paid before it can begin making payments to the common stockholders.

From the investor's viewpoint, there are few advantages to owning preferred stock rather than corporate bonds, as the investment is somewhat less secure. In the event of bankruptcy, bondholders are first in line, before preferred stockholders. Still, advantages may lie in the somewhat higher interest rate over corporate bonds or in the length of time until maturity. Because preferred stocks have no date of maturity, they can be used when you want to lock yourself into a certain interest rate indefinitely. Since a bond is almost always paid off at a specified future date, you can seldom find a bond that goes on paying a specific interest rate forever. The average yields of preferred stocks and corporate bonds for 1965 to 1987 are shown in Figure 8.1.

U.S. Government Bonds and Notes

A short-term *U.S. government note* has less risk than any other form of investment. You have no fear of losing your principal because the U.S. government has to pay it back, and the U.S. government cannot go bankrupt because it has the power to print money. Since a note from the U.S. government is a short-term loan, you don't have substantial risk in terms of fluctuation of market price due to interest rates (which we'll discuss at the end of this chapter).

A *U.S. government bond* is a long-term loan. You lend the U.S. government money that won't be repaid for at least five years to as long as 30 years. These loans return a higher interest rate to the investor than do short-term U.S. government notes. And you can be sure that if you hold the bond until its maturity, you'll be repaid your principal in full.

Municipal Bonds

A *municipal bond* is a certificate signifying a loan to a government entity other than the U.S. government. When you buy a municipal bond you are lending money to a state or local government agency. A municipal bond has greater risk than a U.S. government bond because states and cities do not have the power to print money and have been known to go into default.

FIGURE 8.1   Average Yield of Preferred Stocks and AA Rated Bonds 1965–1987*

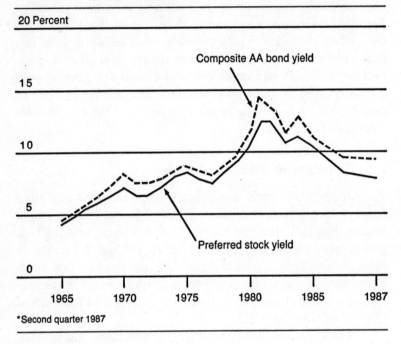

20 Percent

15

Composite AA bond yield

10

5

Preferred stock yield

0

1965   1970   1975   1980   1985   1987

*Second quarter 1987

Municipal bonds have one substantial advantage over U.S. government bonds, however—the interest you collect on municipal bonds is exempt from federal income tax. You do, however, have to pay state income tax unless the bond is from your home state. (States vary on this. A few states charge income tax on municipal bond interest, but most don't. Check with your broker before buying.) With a U.S. government bond you have to pay federal income tax, but not state income tax on the interest collected.

Most municipal bonds are *general revenue bonds*, which means that the city or municipality issuing the bonds guarantees the investors that the interest and principal will be paid back and, if necessary, that the municipality will use its taxing power to obtain those funds. Until the 1970s most investment specialists saw little risk in buying a general revenue bond, because of the city or state's ability to tax people and raise the funds to pay off interest and principal.

Well, times have changed, as became painfully obvious in the mid-1970s when New York City almost defaulted on its loan obligations. New York's situation was typical of many large cities, as migration patterns by middle- and upper-income groups from the cities to the suburbs emerged, leaving behind in the cities a larger and larger percentage of lower-income individuals. The same migration pattern is true for businesses.

To support its services, a city can only tax within its boundaries. As fewer businesses and well-to-do citizens remain in a city and real estate values decline, tax rates must go up for those who are left behind. This has been the pattern in New York City and in the majority of large industrial urban areas. It certainly is not impossible for a city to go bankrupt and this, in fact, was a very real fear for New York.

When you buy state bonds, the risks are somewhat reduced because you have the diversity of counties and cities within state boundaries. The state has the benefit of being able to tax those who fled the city for the suburbs; a city doesn't have that luxury.

Another type of municipal bond is called a *revenue bond*. For example, when New Jersey built its turnpike, it financed the turnpike by selling bonds to the public and promising a certain interest rate on those bonds. The funds to pay that interest came from tolls collected on the turnpike. Often revenue bonds are not backed by city or state governments, but just by a particular project. As a rule, these are successful, but there are numerous exceptions in which the projects didn't raise enough money to pay, in full or in part, the interest on the bonds. In such instances investors may lose part of all of their money.

The 1986 Tax Reform Act eliminated the tax-exempt status for one category of municipal bonds, the industrial revenue

TABLE 8.1   The Two Major Bond Rating Systems: Moody's and Standard & Poor's

Moody's 18 Ratings		Standard and Poor's 11 Ratings	
Aaa1 Aaa2 Aaa3 }	highest quality, least risk	AAA AA A }	highest quality, least risk
A1 A2 A3 Baa1 Baa2 Baa3 }	medium quality, medium risk	BBB BB B }	medium quality, medium risk
Ba1 Ba2 Ba3 B1 B2 B3 Caa Ca C }	lowest quality, highest risk	CCC CC C C1 D }	lowest quality, highest risk

bonds, i.e., bonds issued for private purposes but under municipal government sponsorship. If your goal is to save taxes, be sure to avoid these municipals. You'll notice their interest rates are much higher due to their lack of immunity from federal taxes.

Municipal bonds, like corporate bonds, are rated by Standard & Poor's and Moody's. See Table 8.1. These rating systems attempt to draw fine lines between various bonds, and they are usually right. Keep in mind, though, that one of the reasons I'm writing this book is so you don't entirely rely on professional advice. In the case of New York City municipal bonds, the services didn't have the vision to see that sooner or later, as wealth left the city, the possibility of bankruptcy would loom. It's my own opinion that you didn't have to be an expert to see this possibility; the writing was on the wall for a long time before the crisis. Listen to what the experts say, use their ideas, but don't be afraid to think for yourself.

Zero Coupon Bonds

As discussed earlier, a bond is a loan you're making to the government or to a corporation that pays yearly interest. A zero coupon bond also pays yearly interest, but you don't get it yearly. You get it in one lump sum at the maturity of that bond. With a conventional bond, if a corporation wants to borrow $2,000 from you today and agrees to pay you 14 percent interest, it could pay you $280 per year for a period of time and then pay you back the $2,000. In other words, it could write a 20-year bond and pay you interest yearly plus $2,000 at the end of 20 years. But with a 20-year zero coupon bond at 14 percent interest, you would lend the corporation the $2,000 today and get a lump sum in 20 years. That lump sum would be the $2,000 compounded annually at 14 percent, or a total of $27,948.92.

As great as this sounds, there is one big problem. The IRS says you must pay tax yearly on the income, even though you don't receive it until maturity of the bond. Each year that bond gets more valuable as it approaches maturity, and the IRS says that you're earning 14 percent per year on the value of the bond each year. So the first year you have $280 of income to declare but no cash income from the bond with which to pay the tax. That income will increase each year as the bond becomes more valuable.

Because of this tax problem with zero coupon corporate bonds, they are usually not the appropriate investment for an individual, with one very clear exception: when they are placed in tax-deferred retirement accounts such as IRAs or Keoghs (discussed later).

In these accounts, income is accumulated, but tax is deferred until age 59 1/2 or beyond. Thus, if you buy a 20-year 14 percent zero coupon bond at age 40, when you reach age 60 you would have a $27,948 lump payment made into your IRA and would pay taxes only when you withdraw the interest or principal on that lump sum. Zero coupon bonds and IRAs began at approximately the same time and they are a terrific match. With a zero coupon bond, you'll know exactly how many dollars you'll have in 20 years.

In addition to the benefits of zero coupon bonds when placed in a retirement account, there is another motive for buying them. If you bought a conventional (non-zero coupon) bond today with the belief that it is a good investment because interest rates are historically high and will be coming down, you're faced with one problem: If you're right and rates do decline, you won't be able to reinvest your interest income at a rate as high as 14 percent. With zero coupon bonds reinvestment of income at that profitable interest rate is guaranteed.

The zero coupon bond ensures that your income will be reinvested and compounded at the same 14 percent rate for 20 years, or whatever length your *zero* is. So if you're convinced that interest rates are high now and coming down over the long-term, a zero is a terrific investment, particularly for an IRA.

If you're convinced that interest rates will come down and want to buy a zero, but don't plan to put it in a tax-deferred account, you have another option. Municipal zeros offer an interesting alternative to the non-IRA buyer, particularly if you buy a municipal bond from the state in which you live. That bond probably is not subject to state or federal taxes and, therefore, you do not have to pay any income tax on the income as it's earned, i.e., on income you don't receive until maturity of the bond. The disadvantage is that municipals earn a lower rate of interest because they are free from federal taxes.

Sort of a U.S. Government Zero

Let us say that you think the idea of a zero coupon bond is perfect for you, but you feel a corporate bond is too risky because a corporation could go broke. Ideally, you'd like to get a federal government zero bond. Until 1985 you couldn't, because the federal government didn't issue zero coupon bonds. However, the brokerage firm of Merrill Lynch created an investment vehicle to serve the same purpose, and other firms have followed. Merrill Lynch sells what are called *TIGRs* (Treasury Investment Growth Receipts). From your viewpoint, these perform as if they were government-issued zero coupon bonds. You decide in what year you would like your government bonds to mature and Merrill Lynch accomplishes this for you through a fairly complicated pool arrangement.

For example, in 1985 I asked my broker if I could get a $2,000 zero coupon TIGR maturing in 18 years; my broker said it could be arranged, and the bond would come to maturity at approximately $17,500 in 18 years, with a compounded rate of interest of 12.4 percent. For those of you who aren't comfortable unless you know exactly how Merrill Lynch accomplishes this, the explanation is at the bottom of this page.*

In 1985 Uncle Sam entered the business. Beginning in February, the U.S. government issued its own version of zero coupon bonds, called *STRIPS* (Separate Trading of Registered Interest and Principal of Securities). They are available in face value increments of $1,000—with no commission charge—through stockbrokers, banks and saving and loans. STRIPS may well make TIGRs and the like endangered species. The rates as of this writing are approximately the same as on the comparable TIGR-type investments.

Again, as with every investment vehicle, there is a negative to go with the positive; there's always a price. Should you be unlucky enough to buy a zero coupon bond at eight percent just before the economy enters a period of hyperinflation in which interest rates skyrocket, you're locked into this eight per-

---

*Merrill Lynch will buy, let us say, 20 $1 million government bonds and notes, each one coming to maturity in a different year and each paying semiannual interest. Merrill Lynch will then figure out all the cash coming in from this purchase over the 20 years and will sell distributions of money, i.e., TIGRs, over those 20 years. In other words, it will sell TIGRs so that with the dollars paid out the first, second, ... through the twentieth years, all the money is distributed from this fund of one-year to 20-year bonds and notes. It's kind of a mind twister, but very clever and workable.

cent rate for the whole term of the bond. You could direct that the bond be sold, but you'd suffer a big loss. Potential buyers could earn a higher rate elsewhere and, therefore, would only pay a low price for your bond.

A second risk to avoid is that your zero coupon bond might be *callable*, which means that the issuer has the right to buy it back at a prescribed price at a future date before maturity. If interest rates were to drop dramatically, the issuer might choose to buy it at a slight premium over what it would be worth if interest rates had remained stable. The issuer would do this because it could then borrow money at a much lower rate. The issuer would pay you off and borrow at a lower rate; you would then have to go out and buy another zero or bond at a much lower rate of return. So ask your broker, investment advisor or banker if the zero bond you're buying is callable. You want to make sure that if you've made a wise decision in buying a zero (if you're correct in your belief that interest rates are historically high), you will get the full benefits of your decision and enjoy the use of that zero for the full 20 years.

The biggest risk of all with the zero coupon bond is inflation. Suppose inflation were to accelerate, reach 14 percent, and continue at 14 percent for 20 years. Suppose, also, that you had bought a zero coupon 14 percent bond at $2,000 that matured at $27,948 in 20 years. Your purchasing power at its maturity would be identical to $2,000 today. For you to do well with this vehicle, your return must exceed inflation.

The Interest Rate Risk

When you buy preferred stock or a corporate, U.S. government or municipal bond, you don't have to wait until maturity to sell them. You can sell them on the open market just like you sell common stocks. They fluctuate in price based on three main factors: 1) changes in the safety or prosperity of the corporation or government agency; 2) changes in interest rates; and 3) changes in the rate of inflation.

The main criterion for choosing a corporate bond or any fixed-interest instrument of investment is safety. If, after you buy a corporate bond, the corporation gets into serious financial trouble and you try to sell that bond on the open market, you are likely to get less for it than when you bought it. On the other hand, if the corporation triples in size it does not follow that you are likely to get any more for that bond. Changes in interest rates have the biggest impact on the market price of existing bonds. For example, let's say you have just bought a $1,000 bond that pays $100 a year (ten percent interest) and it will mature in 50 years. One year later the general market interest rates drop to five percent. If you decide to sell your bond, you'll get a lot more for your bond than you paid for it. As a matter of fact, you'll get almost $2,000. Since your bond pays $100 a year, if someone pays you $2,000, he or she will be receiving five percent a year on the money. Of course, in 50 years this person will only get $1,000 back from the corporation, but 50 years is a long time, and that person will be willing to pay almost $2,000 to collect $100 a year for 50 years.

If, on the other hand, interest rates have risen from ten percent to 20 percent, the market value of your bond will have gone way down. The price it brings now will be only about $500, because at $500 a dividend of $100 a year is about 20 percent; thus, an investor will give you $500 to get a 20 percent rate of return. Although the bond at maturity will be worth $1,000, 50 years is a long time to wait for that $500 profit. Therefore, if you believe interest rates are going to rise, don't buy a bond now—wait until interest rates rise. If you believe interest rates are going to fall, however, buy your bond now, before they go lower. If you want to make a capital gain, don't buy a bond that matures in two or three years; instead, buy one that doesn't mature for many years.

Inflation creates a substantial risk in buying bonds. By way of illustration see Figure 8.2, especially the periods 1973–77 and 1979–83. As of July 1987, highly rated corporate bonds were yielding about nine percent. At this rate, if you lend a

FIGURE 8.2   AA Corporate Bond Yield and the Rate of Inflation 1950–1985

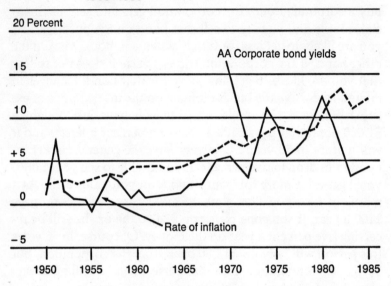

corporation $1,000, it will pay you $90 a year in interest. However, if a substantial rate of inflation exists, even though you're receiving a good interest rate, when you get your capital back at the bond's maturity you will have lost substantial purchasing power. For example, if we continue with a rate of inflation of, let's say, four percent to five percent a year for the next ten years, and at the end of those ten years you get your initial $1,000 back, you won't be able to buy then one-half of the goods you could with that same $1,000 now. Bonds don't represent a hedge against inflation, so the faster prices go up, the more you'll wish you had your money invested somewhere else. Of course, the prices of bonds are affected by inflation. As inflation picks up, people demand a higher interest rate on bonds because they want to be compensated for their loses due to inflation. When these interest rates go up, the market value of bonds that are already issued, are outstanding and are being traded, go down. As inflation abates, the prices of bonds go up because people don't demand as high an interest rate to rent out their money, causing interest rates to subside and bond prices to rise.

Historically, bonds have yielded a "true" rate of three percent. That is, the interest yield less inflation has equalled 3 percent. For example, if a bond were yielding ten percent, you would expect inflation to be at seven percent. A ten percent interest rate less a seven percent inflation rate (erosion of purchasing power) equals a three percent true rate of return.

As inflation accelerated in the 1970s to rates of 12 percent, interest rates moved proportionately to as high as 15 percent to 16 percent on high-grade corporate bonds, yielding a true rate of three percent. The early and mid-1980s saw a rapid decline in inflation, without an accompanying rapid decline in yields on corporate bonds. In 1985, the true yield looked awfully attractive. In January, these bonds yielded 12.25 percent and inflation was running at four percent. By 1987 inflation had dropped below four percent and interest rates to nine percent.

As you read this book, calculate true yields. What is the long-term yield on a high-grade bond and what is the inflation rate? I'd imagine that either the rates are lower or inflation higher than in July of 1987. If the "true" rate is much higher that three percent and you think inflation is not going to accelerate, then bonds are a good buy.

Predicting Interest Rate Fluctuations

When we talk about the rise and fall of interest rates, basically we're talking about the supply and demand for money. The more demand there is for borrowing money and the fewer people or institutions there are who want to lend it, the higher the interest rates will be. When people are less interested in borrowing money and more people or institutions want to lend it, interest rates go down.

The biggest borrowers of money are U.S. corporations and the U.S. government, followed by municipal governments. When the U.S. government spends more on government programs than it receives in taxes, it makes up the difference by borrowing money from its citizens; that is, by selling notes and U.S. government bonds. The larger the budget deficit, the more the U.S. government has to borrow, and the higher the interest it must pay. However, not only do deficits cause interest rates to rise, they also tend to cause inflation. Plus, there is a third side effect: Deficits also tend to cause a shortage of capital. When the government tries to borrow money, it competes with U.S. corporations that need money to expand their present facilities and to grow. The last such tight money situation we had—in 1979—came about because the government had a substantial deficit and had to borrow great sums of money. U.S. corporations, panicked by the fear of double-digit inflation, wanted to borrow as much money as they could to buy inventories and plant equipment before prices got higher. Municipal governments were coming out short; their costs were rising and they needed money to meet their bills. All these groups were competing to borrow money. Consequently, as money became more and more scarce, the prices (interest rates) people were willing to pay to get money went higher and higher.

Where do all these funds come from that are borrowed by corporations and the government? They come from small investors—you and me. They also come from banks, insurance companies, pension funds, foreign investors and foreign governments. The supply of money available for loans is related to how much people earn, how much they put into savings and how much they spend. As earnings rise, there are more funds to be lent out. If people decide to spend a higher percentage of their income and save less, there is less money to be lent out.

Why is it that in 1987, in the face of $200 billion deficits, corporate bonds need to yield only nine percent but they had to pay 16 percent to 17 percent to borrow money in 1979, during that tight money period?

Demand for money, with the federal government borrowing $200 billion, is higher today, but so is the supply of money available to lend. Two major new sources account for this: retirement accounts, including IRAs and Keoghs (discussed later in this book) that create more savings; and a huge influx of foreign investment through sales of U.S. government bonds and corporate bonds. As long as foreigners keep buying our notes (loans), rates could remain stable. But if large deficits continue and foreign investors stop putting their money into our economy, or worse, start selling their bonds, interest rates will skyrocket.

9

Real Estate

Ninety percent of America's millionaires made their money in real estate.

The secret of many fortunes made in real estate is simple: OPM, which stands for *other people's money*.

Successful real estate operators use very little of their own capital in making their investments. Most of the money they use for these purchases is borrowed from savings and loan companies, banks, insurance companies or the seller of the property. For the individual who is anxious to accumulate wealth and who has a small amount of capital—let's say under $10,000—and some time and ambition, real estate is a better vehicle to accumulate wealth than any other I can think of.

Ninety percent of America's millionaires made their money in real estate. Just look around at all the stores, apartment buildings and office buildings. The real estate on any given block is probably worth well over $1 million. If it is not owned by homeowners, local or federal governments or non-profits, it's owned by a landlord who collects rent. Think about it and look around you again.

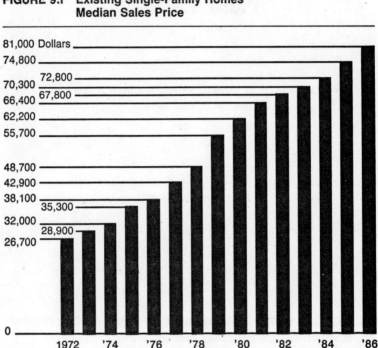

FIGURE 9.1   Existing Single-Family Homes
Median Sales Price

There are three incentives for buying real estate: 1) capital gains—buying real estate at one price and selling it for a greater price; 2) cash flow—the desire to get an annual cash income from rental property; and 3) tax savings. We should be cautious about this last incentive.

Buying a Rental Property

John and Mary are reading the Sunday paper and they notice that someone wants to sell an older duplex—a two-unit apartment house a couple of blocks from where they live. They call about the ad, just out of curiosity. The sale price is $40,000, each flat has six rooms plus a bath, and the building is very run down. They don't know any more about real estate than the average consumer—such as how much people will pay for rent and what people like. They call Friendly Real Estate Brokerage Firm, discuss the property with the broker and make an appointment to look at it. They meet on a bright, cheery Sunday afternoon, look at the property and find it was once a lovely building, but now is run-down, as they were told. The owner, an elderly person, presently lives in the ground-floor apartment but wants to move to a retirement home. The upstairs flat is rented for $150 a month. From the outside it's obvious that the building needs painting; on the inside they find 50-year-old cabinets, original woodwork, hardwood floors that have been scuffed for 30 years without any varnish, wallpapered walls that haven't had a new coat of paint or wallpaper in 40 years and an awful musty smell. They find out a few odd things about the building: There is new wiring, a new roof and a new furnace. All of these were ordered by the city building department on last inspection two years ago. The bathrooms and kitchens have old fixtures, but the water seems to flow well. Viewed as a whole, however, the building looks a wreck.

John and Mary feel somewhat discouraged, so they go out, have a cup of coffee and talk about it. John says, "It's an awfully ugly building." Mary says, "It is, but I can see what it would look like if we could only get in there and fix it up."

"Yeah, but it's such a run-down place. Who wants an old, rotten building that's just going to cause nothing but trouble?"

Mary responds, "Look dear, I was a resident manager of a building before I met you. I know something about real estate. I know that if the roof, wiring, furnace and the plumbing are okay, there's not much else that costs a lot of money to fix. What this building needs is a lot of tender loving care. It needs to be painted and decorated. If we refinished those floors and painted the outside of the building, I think it would be a beautiful, charming apartment house."

John's not convinced yet. He says, "Okay, who's going to do all the work? Will we need to hire someone?" Mary points out they have lots of spare time and they both enjoy painting and decorating. She wants to get started negotiating for the building right away.

One thing that attracts them to this investment is that they know that apartment rentals in that area are relatively high—they are paying $600 a month for their six-room flat just three blocks away from this building. Of course, their flat is lovely and this building is a dump, but it does have great potential.

When John wakes up the next morning, he says to Mary, "We haven't discussed the most important thing."

"What's that?" asks Mary.

"Are we going to make money if we buy this building?"

Mary answers, "I know we can make money, John. I've already figured it out, and here's the story." Mary hands John a piece of paper (see Table 9.1).

As you can see, Mary has calculated what it's going to cost to operate this building—a total of $504 every month. She thinks that they could get the same rent from these two units as they are paying for the one they're living in, if they renovate the way she thinks they should. If they do, they'll make $1,200 a month in rent and have to pay $504 a month to support the building.

"Well," says John, "I see one little problem here—we don't have $40,000 to buy this building."

"That's not a problem, John. We can borrow most of it from the bank. We'll go to a bank or to a savings and loan institution and they'll lend us 80 percent of the purchase price. We just put down 20 percent in cash and the savings and loan institution lends us the rest. The money is handed over to the seller and the savings and loan takes the building as security. If we don't make our monthly payments, the savings and loan will take the building, just like it would take our car if we didn't make our monthly payments on that loan.

"Of course, our costs are going to be higher than $504 a month because we'll have our mortgage payments to make every month, but we'll have 20 years to pay back the mort-

TABLE 9.1	John and Mary's 2-Flat		Monthly Cash Flow		
Rent		$1,200	Net Operating		
Less:			Income		$696
Operating Costs			*Less:*		
(Monthly)			First Mortgage		
Heat	$160		Payment	$320	
Insurance	40		Credit Union		
Water	30		Payment	$150	
					– $470
Electric			Net Cash Flow		$226
(tenants)					
Repairs and					
Maintenance	88				
Bad Debts	36				
Lawn Care	10				
Garbage					
Collection	30				
Advertising	10				
Real Estate					
Taxes	100				
Total Operating					
Costs		– $504			
Net Operating					
Income		$696			

gage. If we put down $8,000 (20 percent cash) we'll have to borrow $32,000, which will cost us about $320 a month to pay back. So we don't need $40,000; we only need $8,000 as a down payment plus approximately another $2,000 for supplies so that I can go in and fix up the building."

John says angrily, "We only have $6,000 in our savings account. How are we going to get $10,000, even if we can borrow $32,000 from a savings and loan institution?"

"It's simple," Mary says. "You can borrow $4,000 from your credit union at work and we can pay them back over three years." She continues as John begins to tremble, less from anger than fear. "If you borrow $4,000 from the credit union and pay it back over three years, we'll only have to pay about

$150 a month. Don't you see, John? We could collect $1,200 a month in rent. Operating the building would cost us $504 a month. Then we would have to pay our $320 mortgage every month. After all that we would still be left with $376 a month. Now the credit union would want $150 a month for the $4,000 loan, but still, that would leave us with $226 a month."

So John gives in and they purchase the building. They fix up the building and get $1,200 a month in rent. They get their mortgage, John gets his loan from the credit union and they now own a building from which they are netting $226 a month in income. That's not bad on a $6,000 down payment.

Mary and John's story illustrates one reason for buying property—cash flow. They are making $2,712 a year in cash from their $6,000 investment, which represents over a 45 percent rate of return. Of course, you must keep in mind this isn't a pure investment; they didn't just write a check and then collect money. It is a combination of a job and an investment. They put a lot of time restoring the building and now they're putting in time receiving calls from tenants, running ads in the newspaper to rent the apartments, paying bills and carrying the burden of an added responsibility. They are also in debt, and for some people that's an uncomfortable place to be.

If John and Mary wanted to, they could achieve another objective of investing in real estate, and that's *capital gains*, or capital appreciation. Their building is worth much more now than the original amount they paid for it. Values in real estate —or at least real estate which serves as income property—are determined in a manner similar to stocks in the stock market: Buildings sell at multipliers of their annual rents. In the stock market, the better the growth potential, the higher the multiplier; whereas in real estate, the better the condition of the building, the newer the building, and the better the neighborhood, the higher the multiplier. In a city such as Chicago, buildings may sell for anywhere from one times annual rent to nine times annual rent. A new eight-unit apartment building in an upper-middle-class suburb, in which tenants pay their own heat and electricity bills, may sell for as high as nine times annual income. A building in a low-income, desolated central-city neighborhood in Chicago, however, may sell for only one times the annual income.

Looking more closely at the building John and Mary bought, we find that in this particular neighborhood, older buildings in good condition are selling for approximately five times their annual rent if the tenants pay their own electric bills. If the landlord pays all utilities, buildings sell for about 4.5 times rent. Obviously, it's better for the landlord if the tenant pays utilities.

One year after buying their building, John and Mary go to a real estate broker and ask what the broker thinks they can get for their building. The broker tells them they could get at least five times their annual rent. Since their annual rent is $14,400, this means they could get at least $72,000, or maybe even as much as $80,000 for their building. The broker asks them to sign a listing contract, promising that if they get the price they want for the house, they will pay the broker a six percent commission. They sign the contract giving the broker the right to sell their house for $80,000 and within one month the broker finds a buyer. John and Mary sell their building for $80,000, pay the $4,800 commission to the broker (six percent of $80,000) and are left with $75,200. They pay off their mortgage, which is $32,000, and they pay John's credit union loan, which is $4,000. As you see in Table 9.2, they are left with $39,200, more than six times their original $6,000 investment. Keep in mind that while the price of the building merely doubled, their wealth increased sixfold. The reason for this good fortune, as we said in the beginning of this chapter, is other people's money.

John and Mary bought the building by borrowing other people's money. Just like margin in the stock market, using other people's money amplifies your gain. However, in real estate you have more control over the value of your building than you do over the market price of a stock. With the excep-

TABLE 9.2   John and Mary's Sale

Sale Price	$80,000
Less Commission (6%)	– 4,800
	$75,200
Less First Mortgage	32,000
	$43,200
Less Credit Union	– 4,000
Total Proceeds	$39,200

tion of rapid neighborhood changes, purchases of real estate seldom go crashing down in value. Usually, if you put any effort into fixing up the building, the value will rise.

John and Mary are now out looking for another building to buy, but this time they'd like to find an eight- or ten-unit building. After they do that, they hope to sell it and find a 30-unit building.

Financing

In the preceding illustration John and Mary needed $6,000 to put their deal together. If they really wanted to take a risk and had no money, but had good incomes and secure jobs, they probably wouldn't have needed *any* of their own capital. They could have borrowed $10,000 from different finance companies or from a relative. This would have put them further out on a limb financially but still able to make the deal. In the securities market it takes money to make money. In real estate, it takes the ability to borrow money (that is, good credit), the will to knock on a lot of doors, the talent to spot a deal that has the potential of increasing in value and a willingness to work pretty hard for a short period of time in order to put all this together.

Most income property and homes are financed either through mortgages or land contracts. A *mortgage* is created when a bank, savings and loan institution or insurance company lends the property buyer 70 percent to 80 percent of the purchase price, and in turn receives anywhere from approximately nine percent to 20 percent interest annually (that is the range in the past ten years), plus the assurance that the loan will be paid back in monthly payments over a 15- to 30-year period. The firm extending the mortgage uses the home as collateral. Therefore, if the payments aren't make, they have the right to foreclose on the home and sell it in order to recover the value of their mortgage.

When money gets tight and lending institutions have less money to pass on the buyers, *land contracts* become more popular. In this case the property seller extends credit to the buyer. For example, the owner is willing to sell his house for $40,000, but the buyer, even though he or she has the $8,000 cash down payment, can't find an institution to give a mortgage for the remaining $32,000. The institutions don't have it, due to a tight situation. Consequently, the seller says to the buyer, "Look, give me your $8,000 as a down payment, and you can owe me the $32,000. You can pay me monthly, just like you would a bank, and at the end of 20 years you'll own the house, and I'll be collecting income for 20 years. After all, if you give me all this cash, I'm just going to put it in the bank anyway and collect income in it. Why shouldn't I collect it this way?"

The land contract is negotiated between the buyer and seller, and when the buyer writes up an offer on the property and hands it to the seller, it's up to the buyer to decide what interest rates he or she is going to offer to pay the seller. Of course it's up to the seller to respond and either accept the deal or counter with a higher interest rate or a higher price than the one offered. It's like negotiating for the purchase of a car or a TV set, except it's a little more formal. Everything is put in writing. The first few times one enters into such an agreement, a lawyer should examine the offer before it is formally submitted.

No doubt a question you will have as you read this chapter is, "But I don't have *any* money, so how can I buy real estate?" Well, a third way to finance real estate is to use a *second mortgage*. Again, we'll use the example of the $40,000 house.

Typically, you'll be able to borrow $32,000 to pay the seller (80 percent of purchase price) from a savings and loan, but you'll still owe the seller $8,000. You can deal with that $8,000 through a second mortgage, *if* the seller is agreeable. During the negotiations, you propose to the seller that you give him an IOU for $8,000 at an attractive interest rate, say 12 percent. That IOU serves as the second mortgage note. As security for the $8,000, the seller has the right to sue you for payment. He can foreclose on the property and receive everything above what the first mortgage holder receives. Under this action, the savings and loan that lend $32,000 on the property will get its full $32,000 before the second mortgage holder gets anything.

To summarize, the seller wound up with $32,000 cash plus and IOU from you, for $8,000. You wound up with a $40,000 building and a debt to the savings and loan for $32,000 and to the seller for $8,000. Your outlay of cash was $0.

Some savings and loans frown on this type of financing, so you might have to do a lot of shopping, but if you have a good job and good credit, you'll probably find a savings and loan that will agree, assuming you find a seller who is willing.

The land contract is simpler than using a second mortgage to obtain financing because there is no institution involved; there is just a transaction between the buyer and the seller. From the buyer's viewpoint, one disadvantage is that if a payment is missed the seller can *foreclose.* In a foreclosure on land contracts, the seller simply takes the property back. If you have made payments on the property for three years and then can't make any more payments, you lose everything. This is different from a mortgage: If you miss your mortgage payments and there's a foreclosure sale, whatever proceeds come from the mortgage sale are first used to pay off the mortgage. Any remaining proceeds are used to pay off a second mortgage, if there is one, and anything left after that is yours. You don't lose the equity you built up in the building, that is, you

TABLE 9.3   Computing Taxable Income

Cash Flow* ($226 a month)	$2,712 a year
Less Depreciation Expense (a noncash expense)	−1,163
	$1,549
Add the amount we reduced our debt last year	
First Mortgage ($30 per month)	$ 360
Credit Union Loan ($100 per month)	1,200
	+ 1,560
Total Taxable Income	$3,109

*All cash is less total monies spent. This figure represents what would go in your pocket each year if there were no income taxes.

don't lose the difference between the market value of the property and what you owe.

Taxes

The main tax benefit in dealing with real estate involves *depreciation*. A building won't last forever. It might last 300 or 400 years, but it won't last forever. Uncle Sam allows you to use this fact when determining your income tax on a building. The example in Table 9.3 involves our rental property, which produces a monthly net cash flow of $226. For the purpose of your income tax, you are allowed to subtract depreciation from this amount.

Uncle Sam calculates that an apartment building will last 27^{1}/2 years; this means that every year you can take 3.63 percent of the cost of that building and subtract it from your earnings. This also means that in 27^{1}/2 years the building technically would be worth nothing.

You don't, however, take the depreciation of the full $40,000, because your local real estate assessor has determined that $8,000 of that amount represents the value of the land upon which your building sits, and the land doesn't depreciate. This breakdown of land/building value is updated yearly and is part of the information on your annual tax bill.

That leaves us with a value for the building of $32,000, and Uncle Sam calculates that it loses 3.63 percent of that value (or $1,163) each year. That amount is called the property's yearly depreciation, and you may deduct it from your rental income. You now have taxable income from the property of $1,549 per year (see Table 9.3). This noncash expense represents a considerable savings to the property owner at tax time.

While the interest portion of your mortgage payment is considered a cost of doing business, the part of your mortgage payment which repays principal is *not*. Therefore, after subtracting depreciation from our cash flow, we have to add back principal reduction on our loans to get total taxable income.

Returning to our example, suppose the mortgage payment of $320 breaks down this way:

> Interest on loan $290
> Repaid principal $ 30

In order to accurately calculate your taxable income on the property, you must add the $30 of repaid principal back to the cash flow. As we see in Table 9.3, you had $360 per year ($30 × 12 months) in principal that you were repaying to the savings and loan holding the mortgage. Another $1,200 per year principal was being repaid to the credit union to reduce that loan. When you add these principal payments back into your expense, you'll end up almost where your started: at $3,109.

Keep in mind that you are making much more than what you are paying taxes on. You are making a cash flow of $2,712 and reducing your debts by $1,560 ($360 + $1,200). Thus, you are really making $4,272 and only paying taxes on $3,109.

There is one problem with this depreciation, however: It will catch up with you when you sell the building. For example, let's say you hold the building for 30 years, pay off the mortgage and sell the building for $40,000, the same price at which you bought it. Uncle Sam says your profit is what you sell the building for, less the depreciated value of the building. Even though you bought the building for $40,000 and sold it for the same price, Uncle Sam says you now have $32,000 capital gain or profit because of the land, or $8,000. If you had sold the building for $80,000, Uncle Sam would say your profit was $80,000 minus $8,000 (or $72,000), rather than the true profit of $40,000. However, you are still a winner in all this because for 30 years you've avoided paying a part of your taxes.

The new tax law does allow you to write off up to $25,000 of real estate operating losses against ordinary income, as long as you earn under $100,000 a year from other sources. Thus, if you only break even on a cash flow basis, at least you'll save something in income tax, thanks to depreciation.

Apartment Buildings: New vs. Old

As mentioned earlier, the newer a building, the higher a multiplier you must pay for it. One advantage of owning a new building, of course, is that it is less difficult to manage. There are fewer mechanical problems and, generally, fewer things go wrong. You're also less likely to have complaints from tenants in a new building.

However, a new building usually yields a lesser cash flow because you are paying a higher multiplier and with a new building there's not much you can do to change or increase its value. An older building, as a rule, has a much greater potential for improvement than does a new one—you can decorate it, paint it, change its character or restore its older character and, thereby, substantially alter its value.

Risks in Apartment Investments

The most frequent mistake I've seen made in income property investment has been underestimating the cost of operation.

Utilities always seem to cost more than expected and repairs and maintenance tend to be volatile budget items. This is particularly true with older buildings.

Many people who own property say, "Well, this year I didn't make any profit, but this year was exceptional, because I had to put on a new roof. And last year I didn't make any money, but *that* was unusual because I went through a city building code inspection and I had to do a lot of things to meet the crazy new requirements." The reality of the matter is, of course, that year after year unforeseen and expensive things do happen to older buildings. Be aware of this and take it into account when you make your plans.

In large cities a very substantial investment risk can be a shift in the composition of the population making up a neighborhood. Real estate values do go down substantially—sometimes drastically—when a neighborhood changes from middle to lower class. In some areas of Chicago, for example, property used to sell at five or six times gross annual earnings, but now many owners are happy if they can sell it for two times gross annual earnings. How can you succeed in a neighborhood where 30 percent or 40 percent of the tenants are unemployed? Many landlords just abandon their buildings and hope that the bank or insurance company won't sue them personally for the mortgage.

Of course, this neighborhood shift can work in reverse and be very profitable. Again, an example can be found in Chicago, in an area now called *New Town*. For a number of years it was run down, occupied by people in the lower-middle income groups or upper-lower-income groups. Gradually the neighborhood started to shift, becoming—because of lower rents—a haven for artists and eclectics. When this happened, other people started buying older buildings in the neighborhood and restoring them. Soon a stream of middle- and upper-middle-income professional people—mainly single—began moving into the neighborhood and values began to soar. Buying real estate in this area just before this trend was like buying stock in a company that no one knew was going to grow and that was selling at a very low multiplier. You didn't have much to lose (the price was already rock bottom), but you could have a lot to gain.

Another risk for the investor is politics. The doomsday bomb to anyone who owns rental property is *rent control* (rents which are frozen at low rates). In real estate you can survive increasing costs and increasing government regulation because as your costs increase, you can pass in most of those increases to tenants through higher rents. But rent control can mean the end of the line. For some apartment building operators in New York City, for example, it has meant slow death. The costs of running and maintaining a building often increase faster than the rents, and sooner or later the landlord has to give up the building (just walk away and abandon it). Statistics show that in the 1980s in New York City, landlords had given up approximately 1,000 apartments a week.

An additional risk for investors is *overbuilding*. In the early 1970s, a lot of money was available nationwide for construction of apartment buildings. Many were built—so many, in fact, that occupancy rates in some areas of cities dropped to 70 percent, and the average *new* apartment complex had about 30 percent of its apartments vacant. In 1983-84, Houston saw a similar overbuilding phenomenon due to overoptimism.

In order to break even, new apartment complexes need about 95 percent occupancy. As a result of the overbuilding there were many bankruptcies nationwide in the 1970s and in Houston in the early 1980s. The oversupply of apartments also had a spillover effect on other apartment buildings, as tenants were lured away to new buildings that had to offer cut rates in order to fill up their apartments.

Changes in local economies also represent risks. For example, the drop in oil prices in 1985–87 caused a large increase in unemployment in Texas, Oklahoma and the entire Oil Belt. Houston, after overbuilding, was hit with this second wallop; by 1987 landlords were trying desperately to give away their buildings for the mortgages. Savings and loans that had to take back apartment buildings that were 50 percent to 70 percent vacant were offering them to investors at cut-rate prices or zero percent interest for one to three years.

Commercial vs. Residential Real Estate

Many real estate investors prefer to be involved in commercial real estate rather than rental housing. Commercial real estate includes stores, factories, warehouses and office buildings. While similar principles of investment apply in both fields, there are greater risks in dealing in commercial property.

In most rental markets you can find someone to whom you can rent an apartment without great difficulty. You might have to reduce the rental price by $10, $20 or $30, but at some point you can rent it and bring in enough money to survive. Even if you lose some money, you can still avoid catastrophe.

But with commercial property there can be long dry spells between tenants. After all, people have to live somewhere, but they don't have to open businesses. And in bad economic times, it might not matter how little you charge for rent; people just might not be opening businesses, period. Think of the stores you've seen with "For Rent" signs in the windows for one or two years. Unless you're a large operator with a lot of other property, it's hard to survive such a long period without any income from rent.

As a result, the default or bankruptcy rate among office and commercial ventures is substantially higher than among apartment buildings. It's also a lot more difficult to get leverage, i.e., to borrow a large percentage of the purchase price. Lending institutions tend to lend only 60 percent or 70 percent on commercial ventures, versus up to 80 percent on an apartment development or acquisition of existing apartment buildings. Therefore, if commercial real estate doesn't offer a higher return on your money than apartment buildings, it is a poor choice, since you should be compensated for higher risks.

As in apartment investing, from time to time there are golden opportunities in commercial investing. You many find, for example, an old mansion in a commercial neighborhood or on a busy street that could be converted to commercial use, but is considered a white elephant, and priced very low. Or you may know of both a vacant warehouse that the owner wants to unload and also a potential tenant. In this case you might make the owner of the warehouse the following offer: He or she will wait 60 days to actually close on the deal and you will meet the asking price. But first you put up only a small amount as *earnest money*—let's say, $500 on $100,000. You also specify that if you don't get a tenant within the 60 days, then you don't have to go through on the purchase, but you will forfeit your $500 earnest money.

If you do find a tenant, you would have him or her sign a long-term (five to 15 years) lease and proceed to close the deal with the seller. You now own a rented warehouse and, since a rented warehouse is often worth twice what a vacant one will fetch when put on the market for resale, you may therefore want to sell your warehouse immediately to take a capital gain. Or, since it is rented, you may want to hold it for purposes of cash flow. Of course, before you embarked on this venture you have already calculated cash flow and found it to be substantial, otherwise you wouldn't have gone through with the deal in the first place. The costs of running a commercial building may be substantially less than an apartment building due to the fact that the tenant usually pays all utilities, and in some cases the contract is to lease net, i.e., the tenant pays taxes, repairs, utilities—everything, in fact, but the mortgage. On the other hand, in an office building where you pay all utilities plus janitorial service, you keep a much smaller percentage of each dollar collected in rents.

Real Estate Investment Trusts

If the risks and effort involved in buying real estate sound too risky or stressful, real estate investment trusts (REITs) might be for you. A REIT is to real estate as a mutual fund is to common stocks. A fund manager buys a group of buildings, be they commercial real estate, apartments or offices, and sells stock in this fund of buildings to individual stockholders such as yourself. You then own a very small portion of a real estate portfolio.

Typically, these REITs that invest in real estate equity put much more down than you might in your hands-on operations. They may put 30 percent or 40 percent down (your money) and borrow 60 percent or 70 percent of the money to purchase these properties. If all goes well, you get a dividend which represents the cash flow in the operations of these buildings. You won't make as much money or make it as fast as you would by buying a building and turning it around yourself, but you will get some of the benefits of real estate ownership, i.e., cash flow and appreciation.

REITs are "tax qualified." If they pay out 95 percent of their earnings to investors, they don't have to pay corporate income tax. For this reason they tend to have higher yields than the average common stock, i.e., they're not reinvesting most of their earnings each year but paying them to you.

Another type of REIT is a mortgage REIT. Rather than investing in buildings, the manager loans money or buys mortgages. This gives a stable, high cash return and indirectly puts you in the lending or banking business. The disadvantage of this type of REIT is that you don't benefit from inflation.

Therefore, if real estate intrigues you but you don't want the hassles, I suggest buying an equity REIT. You can invest as little as $100 or as much as you like by buying stock in these vehicles on the over-the-counter, American or New York Stock Exchanges. Besides less grief, a REIT possesses finally one substantial advantage over buying real estate directly: It is liquid. You can buy and sell your shares like any other common stock.

Master Limited Partnerships

Master limited partnerships (MLPs) have gained popularity since passage of the 1986 Tax Reform Act. They have most of the same characteristics as REITs, with one very important difference. The income from MLPs is considered passive income. Under the new tax law there are three types of income: ordinary income, portfolio income (stocks, bonds, etc.) and passive income. Passive income is derived from "passive" investments, including real estate, limited partnerships, oil limited partnerships and the like, where the limited partners have no management involvement and have limited liability.

These tax-sheltered vehicles no longer provide tax shelters for higher income investors who enjoyed these tax benefits prior to 1986. The paper losses former tax shelters continue to generate cannot be written off against ordinary or portfolio income, but can be written off against positive passive income. MLPs generate positive cash flow, and the income they generate is tax free to the extent that the passive former tax shelters generate passive losses. They are an excellent match for the person who has tax shelters but no longer has sheltered income, and thus is gaining no value out of those shelters.

Following passage of the Tax Reform Act, there was a rush of MLPs to the market. Most were provided by *spinoffs* from existing corporations. For example, a hospital chain might in effect sell twenty of their hospitals to the public and then pay rent on those hospitals. The proceeds it receives from selling the hospitals goes into the treasury of the hospital management company. A fast-food franchise company might sell off a large number of its stores to form an MLP, collecting millions of dollars from the investing public, and in return paying the investing public rent on those restaurant buildings.

While the yields are quite high on MLPs, the quality of that income stream is often questionable. Because investors were very hungry to find companies to give value to their now-valueless tax losses from tax shelters, MLPs were often gobbled up with little thought. Often the market value or price of the MLP would drop dramatically after it was publicly issued.

The point is, when you buy an MLP, be very careful in determining the value of the assets generating your income. Keep in mind that part of the value of a MLP to buyers comes from the tax losses generated elsewhere that they now get an opportunity to use. If you don't have any obsolete tax shelter investments, you don't get that benefit, so you wouldn't get the full value another buyer would get from purchasing an MLP. Also, keep in mind that these particular tax laws are very controversial. Before you invest in an MLP check with your accountant or the IRS for any recent tax law changes.

Real Estate Limited Partnerships

Somewhere in between the risks and rewards of REITs and MLPs and owning real estate directly is the limited partnership. With this vehicle, a managing partner raises money from several investors, anywhere from five to several thousand. Typically, the limited partnership has ten to 35 investors. All become partners and the general partner, who often puts up little or no money, becomes an owner along with the investors in the property. The investors do no work (other than researching the investment) and in most cases have no personal liability on the mortgage, if there is one. The general partner signs the mortgage, assumes the burden of financial risk and has the headaches of operating the properties. Often you can visit the property in question, as it may be in your hometown; perhaps a realtor you know is syndicating a 24-unit apartment house down the block. When you buy shares in a REIT, the properties are usually in several cities and therefore difficult and not worth your time and effort to inspect.

Under the Tax Reform Act of 1986, limited partnerships lost a lot of their appeal and popularity. Until then the general partner took on all liabilities and, even if the buildings broke even, the limited partners received a substantial tax write-off. Under the new law you can only use depreciation for a personal tax write-off when you're personally at risk in a partnership.

Another disadvantage of this vehicle is that it is not liquid. It may be even more difficult to sell one share out of 35 in a limited partnership than to sell a two-flat building. There is often no market for resale of these investments, profits come from cash flow and from liquidation of the partnership when the building is sold.

For investors to get any tax benefits, they must be at risk in the mortgage with a proportionate share of the deal and have some say in the management. This is now being accomplished by a rise in the number of general partnerships. Here, you are a partner (not limited) and liable like anybody else. You may get the benefits of depreciation, but you now have the drawback of greater risk. If you invest in a limited partnership or in a general partnership, make sure you know the property involved and the managing partner and are confident of the value and future of both.

Land

How many times have you heard someone say, "Land is a terrific investment. They're not making any more of it and as a finite commodity, it's becoming more and more valuable." Don't believe it. In America only a little over two percent of the land is in urban areas. The other 98 percent consists of either farmland or just plain open spaces.

When you buy apartment buildings or commercial property, the tenant helps you pay for the costs of that investment. But when you buy raw land, and you pay for it with borrowed money, every month you have to take money from your pocket to make the payment. There is no income from your own pocket to make the payment. There is no income from raw land. If you buy a piece of land for 20 percent down, hold it for seven years and are lucky enough to sell if for double your purchase price, you're probably still not a winner. With inflation, the interest you've paid on the mortgage, and the fact that for seven years your money has been earning no income for you, the cost of holding that property for that time is approximately equal to the profit you'll make on the sale.

If I had to pick the lemon of the year in real estate investments, it would be the purchase of raw land from a real estate development company selling lots on an island, or in a warm climate or in a new skiing area. Most of the prices in these areas are greatly inflated. Also, they are *not* investments. I visited an island off the coast of Florida and was given a tour of the island by a real estate development company that was selling quarter-acre lots for $6,500 each and asking for only ten percent down (these development companies typically do the financing themselves). I asked the sales representative, "What happens if after you buy the lot you want to sell it?" "No problem," the representative said, "it will probably sell at a higher price six months after you buy it." I went to a local realtor on the island who had a lot of listings of land for sale—the same land the development company was selling. The realtor's clients were people who had bought this land and then, for reasons such as divorce or financial hardship, no longer wanted the land, nor could they afford to make the monthly payments. When they went to sell it, they were lucky if they could get $4,000 for each quarter-acre lot or find someone to take over their payments.

For every investment, of course, there are exceptions, and I am sure the real estate development companies could give examples of people who sold property at a much higher price ten years after they bought it. One positive aspect of land purchase is that it's a very simple thing to do—you make your down payment, you send in a monthly check and in 20 years you own the land. But don't count on making a quick profit and don't do it because you want to get rich. If you look at the purchase of such land as a form of personal consumption—a place to vacation or an area of natural beauty that you can have the satisfaction of preserving—then you'll get what you're paying for.

Most of the people who make money investing in land are those who subdivide or develop. Shortly after buying it, they parcel up the land into smaller pieces and sell it to other people who want to build homes, or in some cases they make industrial parks out of a large piece of land. Occasionally people buy a big piece of land and get very lucky: For example, after they buy the land a shopping center will be built next door, or they discover the land is in the growth development pattern of a spreading metropolis. The latter instance is exemplified by the experience of one of the wealthiest people in show business, Bob Hope. He invested large sums in land that was directly in the future growth patterns of southwestern cities.

Condominiums

A condominium is a type of real estate in which you alone own part and part is shared property. For example, if you bought a *condo* apartment in a high rise, your condo apartment is exclusively owned by you, but the lobby, pool and other general areas are owned in common with all other condo owners. The expenses on the common areas are shared by all owners, but you pay the expenses within your unit. The broad issues in buying a condo as your primary residence are quite similar to those of buying a house and will be taken up when we deal with home ownership.

Resort Time-Share Condominiums

If raw land is termed a poor investment vehicle, then resort time-share condominiums are a disaster.

A time-share condo usually involves splitting one apartment into 52 interval condominium ownership entities. In other words, you buy ownership of one week of the year for perpetuity (or a specific length of time: 25- to 40-year ownerships are typical) of one specific apartment in a condo project in a resort area.

For example, recently I was subjected to an almost unbearable sales pitch for a Florida time-share condo. (The inducement was free 7 × 35 binoculars for just visiting the project—I was underpaid.)

The deal offered was that for $12,500 I could own one week a year (any winter week I chose) for the rest of my life at this condo project. The apartments were nice two-bedrooms, furnished and in a pretty setting. I would shell out this cash and then be assured of inflation-free trips for the rest of my life (at least at the same place and same time each year.)

The costs would also include paying my share of maintenance on the unit plus my share of the ongoing costs of the project: about $300 a year.

What's wrong with this proposition? A lot. First, if you put $12,500 here, you are losing the potential income on that money. At the time of this writing, that would amount to approximately $1,200 a year if invested in government bonds. Secondly, this $300 yearly fee is just for starters. Developers often keep their fees very low when they are selling their units. After they are all peddled, the owners (you) form an association and vote on upkeep costs. These costs can rise dramatically once the developer no longer subsidizes costs, and also as the units start to age. These costs may rise as fast or faster than inflation.

Certainly you are buying some real estate, but you are also buying a lot of marketing costs. For example, recently I spoke with the owner of a modest 40-unit resort in Wisconsin. He said he would gladly sell the resort outright for $800,000 ($20,000 a unit). However, he'd been approached by a time-share marketing firm which wanted to time-share his resort. They would attempt to sell time-share weeks (interval ownership) for $4,000 to $8,500 a week. The total price he would then receive for his 40 units (before paying commissions and marketing costs) was $13,000,000. (He didn't do it because the marketing firm wanted large up-front fees and didn't guarantee results.)

The point is that with time-share resort condominiums, although you are paying for some real estate, you're also paying for a lot of hype. In addition, the cost of ongoing ownership is usually more than expected and the resale weak.

In *The Wall Street Journal* and *U.S.A. Today* time-share foreclosures are for sale frequently and often at 25 percent to 33 percent of the original asking price.

The extremely high-pressured sales tactics that accompany the sale of these deals should be your red flag: Investors Stay Away. If you are considering buying a unit, ask other owners how they have experienced this purchase. Also, check to see if there is an on-site resale program. Keep in mind that if you need to liquidate and there is no specific resale program, you may be competing with the developers in selling your unit —and you won't be able to match their sales efforts.

The purchase of a time-share resort condominium can make sense if you review it as a fun consumption, but don't ever buy the hype that resort time-share condos will certainly go up in value and can only make money for you. That could happen, but the odds aren't with you.

Homes and Condominium Homes

Buying your own house is an excellent investment if home prices in general rise rapidly after you buy it. In the mid- and late-1970s, this was certainly the case.

Although rates of home appreciation vary from region to region, in the past 12 years, nationwide, homes have more than doubled in price. They were an excellent investment if you bought in 1975 and held to 1987 (or 1980, for that matter).

If home prices don't rise after you buy your house, it is a poor investment. In 1981–87, the rate of increase in home values slowed and in some regions homes are selling at prices no greater in 1987 than they were in 1981.

Home ownership is costlier than most people expect. Examining the costs of ownership will reveal why this is true. By mid-1988 the average existing home price will be approximately $95,000. If you pay this (and you can adjust these figures proportionately with your price) and purchase your home with conventional financing, the following will approximate your costs:

Price	$95,000
Less Down Payment—20%	– 19,000
Mortgage on Home	$76,000
Down Payment	$19,000
Plus Point, Fees, Closing Costs*	+ 1,500
Total Cash Out-of-Pocket	$20,500

Monthly Ownership Costs—A $95,000 Home

Taxes	$ 240
Insurance	25
Water	25
Heat & Electric	200
Repairs	100
Replacements & Improvements	240
Lawn & Landscaping	30
Miscellaneous	30
Costs before Mortgage	$890
Plus 20-year Mortgage at 11%	+784
Total Out-of-Pocket	$1,674

Most first-time home buyers and almost all real estate salespeople would say costs are not really this high on repairs and replacements. Well, I believe experience supports my case. From time to time, homes require major injections of capital for new roofs, busted furnaces, exterior painting, new storms or screens, etc. In addition, it's human nature for people to alter things in their homes, to decorate, to recarpet, retile and/or give the house a new look. It's quite easy to spend $4,000, $5,000 or $6,000 for what was thought to be a small project.

---

*Lending institutions charge from one percent to three percent of loans as fees for 20-year conventional mortgages. Also, legal fees, title fees, etc. are incurred at the closing.

A rough approximation of cost (before tax benefits) of home ownership, assuming conventional 20 percent down and 11 percent financing, is 1.75 percent a month of the price of the home. You may not spend this every year, but you should budget it and save the dollars from the years you spend less. You'll need them in the years when everything seems to go wrong at once.

There are tax benefits to home ownership. Real estate taxes and interest on your mortgage are deductible from your taxable income.

Returning to our example and assuming you're in a 28 percent tax bracket, your net cash cost of ownership would be:

Initial Out-of-Pocket Monthly	$1,674
Less Tax Savings	
28% × $240 (Real Estate Tax) =$67	
28% × $697 (Interest on Mortgage) = 195	
Net Reduction in Income Tax − 262	
Net Cash Cost of Home/Monthly	$1,412

It costs $1,412 a month, after tax benefits, to live in this home. To this you must add the cost of the *use* of your down payment. You could have invested that outlay of $19,500 and it would be earning income. Had you invested in U.S. bonds, you would have received approximately 9$^{1/2}$ percent, $1,950 a year, or $163 a month. After tax on that interest (28 percent tax rate) you would keep $117 per month. Therefore, it costs $1,412 plus $117, or $1,529 a month in out-of-pocket, after-tax dollars to live in that home.

Now you would have to rent if you didn't own a home, so we should guesstimate a rent rate to see how much your net home ownership costs. You know your community and rents best, but based on my own experiences, an average home can be rented for much less than $1,529 a month. A $550 to $950 rent would hit most market rents. If we take the average of $750 rent (and here you must plug in rents in your community), then home ownership costs net $1,529 – 750 = $779, or about $9,300 a year more than renting.

If you were buying a home strictly as an investment, would you rent or buy? If you rent and set aside that same amount ($1,529 a month) for housing costs, you would stash $9,300 a year into a savings ($1,529 – 750 = $779 a month × 12 months = about $9,300). In seven to eight years, with compound interest, you would have a $100,000 nest egg, plus the $20,500 you didn't put down on the home, which equals $120,500. To do as well with your home investment, your home would have to have appreciated from $95,000 to $200,000. It would have to more than double in eight years.

All this does not mean you should avoid home ownership. A home provides much pleasure. It provides forced savings, since after 20 years, if you stay in your home, you will own it outright. If home prices double, you will do well financially, and have avoided rising rents elsewhere.

If inflation accelerates and reaches double digits as it did in the late 1970s, home ownership is a good investment. However, owning a home in a period of level prices is a poor investment and though it beats throwing your money down a hole, you could accumulate wealth much more quickly elsewhere.

One final note of caution. If you plan on staying in a community or a neighborhood for only two or three years, home ownership is not prudent. When you sell a home, transaction costs are high. Typically, a broker gets a six percent commission from the seller and the lender gets one percent to three percent of your mortgage when you pay it off. If the value of your home rose, let's say from $90,000 to $100,000 in two years, all your profit would be eaten up in transaction costs. You haven't had time to pay down your mortgage and allow inflation to really work for you.

Condominium Homes

All the preceding information applies as well to condos. However, there are some added financial risks connected with condos.

The biggest risks occur when the condominium project is first offered to the public, and this is true whether it's a converted apartment building or a brand-new project. Looking at it from the developer's side will help you better understand your own risks.

Let us say a developer buys a 20-unit apartment building for $800,000, or $40,000 per apartment. He or she invests another $200,000 in the building to add individual heating and air conditioning, a new lobby, new appliances and to generally upgrade the property. The developer now has $50,000 per unit invested and offers them to the public for $75,000 (not an unusually high markup, since marketing costs are high). He or she quickly sells 12 units to 12 people who rented nearby and were eager to live and own there. The next two sales are rough, as the supply of eager prospects has run out. The developer has now sold 14 units at $75,000 and grossed $1,050,000, but because $50,000 was spend on advertising and sales people, the developer has really only recovered his or her $1,000,000 investment. Let us also add that you are one of the 14 buyers. Well, you could be in a bit of trouble.

Sales are now tough, since the developer has run out of the easy, eager, first buyers, but whatever he or she gets now is profit. After a month of no sales, the developer cuts the price to $70,000, sells two more, then cuts to $65,000, sells one, and finally sells the last three at $58,000, which is $17,000 less than you paid.

At the moment of the last sale, your condo is worth $58,000. You bought it with $15,000 down, but because it's now worth $17,000 less than you paid for it, your equity is now –$2,000. It very well may rise again, but if you have to sell at the same time that the developer is offering the last units at low prices, you run the risk of losing a lot of money.

This scenario is not always the same, but it does happen. If you buy a condo from a condo resident, you avoid this risk. Sometimes it does work in reverse. In boom times, the first buyer may pay less than the last. However, when the salesperson for a new project says to buy now because next month the prices are going up five percent, don't bet the ranch on that future price increase.

Whether you're buying a single-family home or a condo, don't sign before you see a lawyer, a professional who has substantial real estate law experience. Also, don't accept standard guidelines as to how expensive a home you can afford. Real estate salespeople or bankers may use the common guideline that you can afford 2.5 times your annual income in a purchase price. In other words, a person or family making $32,000 could afford our $80,000 house. I think they are being too optimistic. Two times income is a more reasonable guideline for home price, but don't even rely on that. Figure out the realistic costs of home ownership and then decide if you feel your prospective home fits your pocketbook.

Summary

Buying older residential properties with other people's money is the best route for a person without much capital. With patience, some ambition and the courage to take financial risks, it can be the road to creating wealth. As long as inflation continues, prices of property will rise.

As an investor in income property, you will not only get the benefit of rising prices, but the benefit of leverage as well. This means that if a property you bought for $100,000 with $10,000 cash down increases in value by ten percent, your equity will increase in value by 100 percent. With income property—unlike your own home—the tenants pay your holding costs and buy the building for you.

Of course, there are problems with owning real estate, and there are risks: Your property can be a headache and a nagging responsibility and you have the major problem of lack of liquidity—you simply can't sell real estate as readily as you can securities. But if you're hungry enough, it's usually the best game in town.

10

Franchises and Small Businesses

Don't buy a small business or a franchise and think it's just an investment. Remember, you're buying a job.

Sometimes we learn from our mistakes. You're about to learn from mine at no cost to you.

I was in my Mustang convertible, hotfooting it for the state line. I knew that as soon as I crossed it I'd feel a great surge of relief, safe in the knowledge that no creditors could pursue me. You see, I had started out as a silent investor in a franchise, but unfortunately had allowed myself to be drawn into managing the franchise, and now, following its demise, was trying as quickly as I could to run away from the situation. The story I'm about to tell is true, but the names have been changed to protect the guilty, the innocent and me.

Some years ago, I thought *franchising* was the wave of the future for American free enterprise. I saw that it was getting tougher and tougher for small businesspeople to make it on their own. In the franchising system I saw a new sort of compromise between the large and small business, combining the best parts of both.

In researching franchising I came across a large company that offered what seemed like a promising deal. This company ran computer schools. It taught people, for a fee, how to be computer operators. For a charge ranging from $25,000 to $100,000, the company would allow you to become an investor in its franchise: This meant you could use the company's name and expertise and the company would aid you in setting up your own computer school in the city of your choice (the larger the city, the higher the fee). In addition, I found a sales representative for the parent company who was interested in opening up his own franchise. In fact, he had the rights to the very last franchise available in the United States. The necessary capital, including the franchise fee and the money needed to physically open the business, was about $30,000. Since the city in question represented a very small marketing area, all the company required was an initial $10,000 franchise fee plus the $20,000 cash needed for both building alterations to make it suitable for use as a computer school, and operating capital.

The only problem the sales representative for the parent company was having in starting his business was a lack of money. Being a "shrewd" wheeler-dealer, I offered the sales representative $28,000 in cash if he'd come up with $2,000, and for that $28,000, a couple of partners and I would get a two-thirds interest in the school. It was agreed that we'd get paid back our $28,000 out of the first $28,000 in profits earned by the school. From that point on the sales representative would be a one-third owner and we'd be two-third owners. It was especially nice because we'd have nothing to do with the operation of the business. We could just sit back and collect out profits. He agreed. So we sent him the money and in return we received some contracts, and he set up his business. About once a month I would call this fellow to see how things were going. After about eight months I got tired of hearing the same phrase: "I think I can see the light at the end of the tunnel."

A partner and I went out to visit the school. We found 17 students were enrolled, which would have been fine except the business required about 100 students just to break even. Out of the $20,000 in operating capital the sales representative had had six months earlier when he started the business, only about $3,000 remained, and there was about $10,000 in outstanding bills. We also found there were four other established private computer schools in the area, plus a junior college offering an excellent computer program course for about $30 a year. When we discovered that this sales representative had never put his $2,000 into the school in the first place, that he was seldom around and that even when he was around he wasn't working very productively, we asked him to resign and turn over the assets of the company to us. When he refused, we threatened to call the district attorney, whereupon he immediately signed over the assets to me and my by now not-so-silent partner.

As soon as the manager left, we looked at each other and asked, "Who's going to be the new dean of the computer school?" Since my partner had to leave the next day to oversee a franchise employment agency we owned together (an agency in which we were both about to lose our entire investments), there was only one answer to that question. My term as computer school dean is something I still remember vividly, no matter how hard I try to forget.

My first step in attempting to salvage the school was to visit with the parent company, the officers of which offered me a great deal of sympathy. They said, however, there wasn't much they could do to help. It was a bad site selection and the school should never have opened in the town in the first place. I angrily asked them, "Why the hell did you sell it to us?" They said the previous manager had simply insisted. After my visit they did send down a sales supervisor to show us how to recruit students. At the end of six weeks we had recruited one more student.

During those weeks I worked about 14 hours a day, trying to figure out what computer schools were all about and trying to breathe some life into a dying enterprise. At the end of that time I had barely enough money to meet the last payroll. It obviously was time to make a decision: either to inject more capital into this business or to give it up. As this was a corporation, we (my partner and I) weren't legally liable personally for any of the school's debts. We really had tried our best to make it go, but it became obvious there was no need for an additional private computer school in the area.

I talked to two lawyers. The first suggested that I stay, call the creditors and tell them that we were not going to be able to pay the bills—in other words, be very honest. This attorney had recently graduated from law school and was 26 years old. I also talked to an attorney from my hometown, a man with 35 more years of experience, who had seen the ups and downs of hundreds and hundreds of enterprises. He made a most shocking suggestion. He said, "Dick, tonight after you meet your last payroll, lock the door, and get into your car and get out of that state. You're not personally liable for any of those debts, but if you meet with the creditors, they may try to sue you anyway and keep you in the state for years, tied up in the courts. They won't get anything, but they might cost you a lot of money and an awful lot of grief."

So here I was, someone with only the best intentions, who had invested $10,000 of his own money as a silent partner in a computer school—a school aimed at helping young people without careers find a place in society. Here I was, taking this older attorney's advice, getting into my car and heading for the state line. I had done the best I could to reduce the damage to the students by finding another private computer school to take over their program. That school had compensated me by giving me some postdated checks as commission for referring the students. It was hoped that at least these checks would help pay any legal fees if we were sued. As it turned out, the checks were all bad.

The same partner and I proceeded to lose $10,000 in the aforementioned employment agency that was managed by someone else, but I was luckier with a franchise restaurant where I only lost about 40 percent of my investment. Somehow these businesses just never seemed to work out the way their pro forma statements indicated they should. I'm telling you this story in an effort to fill you with a sense of caution that I feel is appropriate to investing in franchises, particularly as a silent investor.

I was a novice when I started in franchising, 25 years old and a little naive. I'm not anymore. While these experiences were a bit extreme, they do point out some useful examples to help you avoid peril. Franchising, however, can be quite profitable and provide you with a direction, income and career. I believe that it *is* possible to succeed with a franchise operation, but there are a lot of factors to consider.

The basic idea of franchising is that the parent company, the franchisor, has expertise in a particular product or area of business. However, due to a lack of either personnel or capital necessary to bring that product or service to more distant areas, the parent company can't develop or distribute this product as fully as it might.

You, a small businessperson, want to own a small business, but don't have the expertise of the franchisor. Therefore, you join forces: The franchisor shows you how to set up your business and operate it and in return you pay a fee and a percentage of your continuing sales. It is hoped that the franchisor has been involved previously in similar operations and you can benefit from the mistakes the parent company has made. You may also benefit from the recognition a well-known name brings to the franchise, such as Kentucky Fried Chicken or Midas Muffler, so that you don't have to spend a long, arduous promotion period familiarizing people with your product. The most important thing to keep in mind when thinking of investing in a franchise is that, unlike investing in stocks and bonds, you are buying a small business. Remember, when you're buying a small business, you're buying a job—small businesses do not make money when left to run by themselves.

There are many franchises that are offered by honest, competent parent companies. On the other hand, innumerable franchising companies also are selling franchises of dubious value. These latter firms are likely to renege on their promises of continuing supervision and help.

While the failure rate of small businesses is extremely high (four out of five small businesses fail within five years after opening), the failure rate for franchises is much lower, This difference is primarily because with franchises you're getting marketing help from people with experience—help in site selection and capital planning. Small businesses fail most often because of poor management; unfortunately, people who start small businesses don't seem to know much about running businesses. They also frequently fail because of inadequate capitalization —the owners just don't have enough money when they open to survive through the rough times of a beginning operation. All these risks are greatly reduced when you buy the franchise.

One of the disadvantages of buying a franchise rather than opening your own small business is that you are paying a substantial *franchise fee*, money the parent company receives for helping you with your site selection, for allowing you to use its name in your business and, frequently, for using its architectural plans to build your facility. As a rule, you'll also have to pay a continuing royalty to the franchisor (a percentage of sales). In a way, this makes it even harder to succeed than it might be with your own business. For example, in the restaurant business, if five percent of your gross sales income goes to the parent company, while it may not sound like a lot, it may ultimately represent half of your total profits. If you sold $100,000 worth of food, then subtracted the cost of food, rent, labor, etc., you might be left with only $10,000 in profit. Paying the parent company $5,000 of that can be distressing.

Some advice: If you're thinking of buying a franchise, talk to a lot of other people who have bought that same franchise. Ask about their experiences in dealing with the parent company and public. Be sure the product you're selling isn't just a fad. Check out competing franchisors with similar services or products before you sign any papers, plus never sign anything before showing it to your attorney. Know that if you *do* invest as an owner-manager, you're also buying a job, and you might have to work 70 hours a week to make the whole thing work.

Finally, as I learned with some pain, don't invest as a silent partner in franchises unless you're willing to take the substantial risk of losing your capital.

There are numerous franchise success stories—people who have bought Kentucky Fried Chicken franchises or Mc-Donald's, and were later bought out by the parent company, becoming millionaires in the process. For every example like this, however, there are probably five sad stories of disappointments, frustrations and financial failures as a result of entering this field.

Small Businesses: Labors of Love

Some advice for those thinking about opening a small business: Most people who have owned their own businesses will admit they probably would have made more money working for someone else at an hourly wage. The reason for this is that most small businesses prove to be marginal operations that require long hours on the part of the owner in order to make ends meet.

If you are determined to open your own small business, do as much reviewing as you can of the competition. If they are similar businesses, try talking to the owners about how they do financially, what kinds of hours they put in and what kinds of volumes they deal in. Try to find out what their biggest headaches are and what their greatest disappointments have been in operating their businesses.

If, as you read this, you're thinking such an investigation would require a lot of assertive behavior on your part, and if you feel uncomfortable at the prospect of being that assertive, then you probably shouldn't even consider opening a small business. Assertiveness and hustle are extremely important ingredients if your business is going to be successful. Seldom are small businesses successful simply because everything went smoothly. In nearly all situations there seem to be unforeseen problems and it always requires a special element of push and drive to make the business successful.

While most franchises require substantial capital from the purchaser, small businesses don't necessarily require a lot of money to open. *Keep in mind that the less you invest, the less you have to lose.* Service businesses, such as travel agencies and real estate brokerage firms, can be opened for the cost of a desk and the installation of a telephone. The small capital investment doesn't mean you aren't going to have a profitable business. It does mean, though, that your business will depend on your own personality, abilities and drive. This is often true as well with small businesses that require substantial initial capital.

Whether you're buying a franchise or opening your own small business, it's important that you do your homework. The Small Business Administration, an agency of the federal government, can offer substantial aid and information to somebody planning to open his or her own business or to buy a franchise. This agency publishes a substantial amount of literature on the subject and the advice is free. If you're not an experienced businessperson, get all the advice and help you can from friends or relatives who do have experience in business. Don't be afraid to talk about your ideas—it's very unlikely that someone is going to steal them. If you don't have business experience, at least talk to people who do or read books on the subject or do both. Otherwise, there is almost a 100 percent chance that you and your small business will fail.

Colleges often offer extension courses on small business. It is a very wise investment of your time to take such a course, which should include the business plan, marketing, bookkeeping, sales, employee relations and finance. Usually, these courses are offered in the evenings or on weekends and take from ten to 20 class hours. I strongly advise you to enroll in such a course before you embark on this adventure.

Compared to buying an apartment building, investing in a small business almost seems like throwing your money away.

The rate of failure, or bankruptcy, in buying apartment buildings is one out of 1,600; this means that less than .1 percent of apartment buildings don't make it. The failure rate in setting up small businesses is four out of five. The amount of time put into running an apartment building is very small compared to the amount of time put into operating a small business. However, a small business can make a handsome living for someone who's talented and successful. Smaller investments in apartment buildings can provide some income, but not the income of a very successful small business.

In summary, if you're thinking of opening up a small business, the following should be your ingredients: 1) you have adequate capital, not only to open the business, but to sustain it for one to two years while it's losing money (and it probably *will* lose money at first); 2) you personally have garnered adequate management experience working for another company or another small business, or you've done substantial research and have the help of somebody who does have managerial experience; 3) you have researched the business and you believe there's a demand for it—you've talked to other people in the business and to your competitors; 4) you're going to really enjoy working 60 or 70 or 80 hours a week; 5) you have an assertive, go-getting personality. If you possess all these ingredients, then you have a good chance of making it. You don't have to be *great* at all of them, of course, but if any one is missing, your chances of success are significantly reduced. If you feel you're lacking some of these personality characteristics, but you have some money to invest, a franchise may be a better alternative. Although you still will have to put in long hours, your own imaginative abilities and creativity are not as essential, since your marketing program is for the most part already planned for you. Above all else, don't buy a small business or a franchise and think it's just an investment. Remember, you're buying a job.

11

Commodities: For the Lover of Risks

Unlike buying and selling common stocks, playing commodities is not an investment. It is speculation.

If you're the impatient type and find boring the idea of making an investment and then waiting two, three or four years before reaping your rewards, commodities might be the game you'd enjoy playing. Commodities are not an investment; they involve too much speculation to qualify. Those who play the game must be willing to lose all the money they invest, but win or lose, they'll know the results within one day to six months. The profits can be 100 percent, 200 percent, even 2,000 percent more than the money you invest—but so can the losses! So if playing this game seems to be more complicated—and difficult —than buying common stocks, you are right. To be good at the commodities game, and to win at it, requires a lot more diligence and a lot more risk taking than playing the stock market.

The following illustration will help you understand the function of the commodities market. A farmer is just planting the seed for his or her wheat crop and this year has put a lot of

147

money into it. The farmer is tired of having to live with all the fluctuations in price; this year he or she would like to know ahead of time what price the crop will bring. Right now wheat might be selling at $2.30 a bushel, but it will be four months until the harvest and the crop is ready to sell. If it's still selling then at that price, the farmer will be all right. He or she will be able to pay all the bills, buy clothes and food, even afford a family trip to California. If the prices goes up to $2.60 a bushel, of course the farmer would be even happier, but if, four months from now, he or she has to sell at $2 a bushel, the farmer won't be able to pay the bills. So the farmer begins to suffer from insomnia, because he or she just doesn't want to take this kind of risk.

Then one day someone knocks at the farmer's front door and says, "I'm from Chew & Chew Wheat Company. We make breakfast cereals and we're getting tired of the fluctuation in prices for the wheat we have to buy. We noticed that you just planted your crop and we would like your promise to sell it to us four months from now when the crop is harvested. We'll promise to pay you the present price of $2.30 a bushel, if you promise to deliver us the wheat for that price at harvest." The farmer likes the sound of the deal, so they shake hands and thereby consummate a *futures contract*.

The farmer is now guaranteed a price at which he or she can make a profit and the cereal manufacturer has nailed down the price that it will have to pay for wheat. That is the simplest possible example of the basic function of the commodities market. The market guarantees a specific price to the farmer now, as well as to the users of the farmer's products later, taking the risk of price fluctuation out of both of their businesses.

Today you can walk into your stockbroker's office or into a company that specializes in dealing in commodities and buy what's called a contract to receive, for example, 40,000 pounds of cattle or 30,000 pounds of cocoa or some amount of some other commodity such as hogs, potatoes, soybean meal, etc. The person selling you the contract guarantees to deliver that amount of product to you at a specified date in the future. The date can be 30 days, 60 days or six months from now. The reason for making such a deal is you may think wheat, for example, is going to be much more expensive six months from now than it is today. So you go to your stockbroker's office, place an order to buy a contract to receive 5,000 bushels of wheat and hope to make a lot of money. If your prediction is right and the market price of wheat rises, then your contract is extremely valuable.

Let's say, for example, that you buy 5,000 bushels of wheat at $2.30 a bushel and the price rises to $2.80 a bushel. You will make a fair amount of money. On the other hand, if the opposite happens—the wheat goes down to $2 a bushel over the next six months and you promised to buy it for $2.30 a bushel—then you're a loser. The winner is the person who sold you the contract, who, by the way, is not likely to be a farmer or someone who really possesses the wheat, any more than you really want delivery of the wheat (only one percent of all commodity contracts actually turn into physical delivery of the commodity). The person who sold you the contract is hoping the price of the commodity is going to go down and you're hoping the price will go up. In effect you're betting against each other as to the future price of wheat.

One reason for all the activity in this game is the low *margin requirement*—often as little as five percent of the total price of the contract. For example, today you may be able to buy a contract for someone to deliver to you 40,000 pounds of cattle. At 66 cents a pound for cattle on the hoof, that would be $26,400 worth of cattle. However, you only need to put up $1,320 in margin to buy that $26,400 contract. Consequently, if the price of cattle goes up from 66 cents to 68 cents a pound, this means you will have made an $800 profit on your $1,320 cash investment (two cents × 40,000 pounds). If the cattle go up to 70 cents, you will have doubled your money. Of course, there's always the chance that events may go the other way. In fact, all that has to happen is to have cattle go down three cents

a pound in price, and you're wiped out. Even if cattle go down
two cents a pound in price you'll be getting a call from your
stockbroker saying that you must come up with more cash for
a down payment or your position on the contract will be sold
out. Therefore, as you can see, the price of a commodity
doesn't have to move very much in either direction in order for
it to have a great impact on you, the speculator.

These low-margin requirements are exciting, but they
weigh heavily against most speculators. Suppose you invest
$1,500 in margin as just described. It's likely that while you
hold that contract, the price is going to go both up and down.
When the price goes up, you'll be ecstatic, but when the price
dips below your cost, you're likely to say, "I can't afford the
loss. Sell my contract, I don't want to come up with more
money." Only if the price goes straight up from the time you
buy it can you avoid at some point being put in a losing position. It takes a lot of capital and courage to back up your com-
mitments in commodities and things often fall before they rise.
This situation is, of course, quite different from the stock market. If you buy a stock at $20 a share and you believe that ulti-
mately it will go to $50, you can just wait while the stock falls
to $19, $18 or even $15, secure in your belief—hopefully well-
founded—that someday the market will adjust to what you see
as the true value.

It's even possible to lose more than you originally put up
in commodities, because it's possible that before your broker is
able to sell your contract, you've lost more than the entire margin amount you invested. In most commodities there is a legal
daily trading limit on the price. In cattle, for example, the limit
to the allowed price fluctuation is 1.5 cents per pound per day.
However, if some significant news causes people to decide that
cattle is worth much less—news such as a famous scientist al-
leging that growth hormones given to cattle cause cancer in
people who eat beef—then even though the price of cattle can
drop only 1.5 cents per pound in a day, your broker might not

be able to sell the contract that day. There have been times when, during a particularly wild market for a commodity—something bordering on a panic—sellers had to wait six or seven days while the commodity continued to drop before they could sell their contract. Most of the time, of course, you only risk the cash you put up, but on occasion you can get stuck in a fiasco like this. Table 11.1 illustrates the cost of one contract in various commodities, the amount you would have to invest and the potential daily and five-day maximum possible gain or loss.

Earlier I mentioned the commodity *seller* who was a farmer. If you think the price of a commodity is going to go down and you want to try to make money on this downward price shift, you can sell a contract that you don't own in that commodity, even though you're not a farmer, in the hope of buying it later at a lower price. For example, if you think that the price of cattle will go from 40 cents a pound down to 35 cents a pound, then you can sell a contract in cattle at 40 cents a pound and, when the price does drop to 35 cents, you can buy a contract at that price, hand it to the person who bought at 40 cents and get off the hook. The scheme works the same way as selling short in common stocks.

Unlike buying and selling common stocks, however, playing commodities is *not* an investment. It is speculation. An investment is something you buy for the future—whether a year or a lifetime. Commodities are usually short-term transactions that are completed in less than six months. You cannot buy wheat or cattle contracts five years into the future; they are all under one year away. Also, you're usually not betting on long-term growth trends the way you would in the stock market; commodity prices continually move up and down.

The fluctuation in prices is the result of supply and demand. Increasing technology usually means higher crop yields and, therefore, a greater supply. Droughts, freezes and other weather conditions can have a huge impact on supplies. In-

TABLE 11.1   Standard Commodity Contracts

Commodity (One Contract Equals)	Cost per Bushel or Ounce 9/17/87	Total Value of Contract	Cash Required to Buy Contract*	Daily Limit in Price Movement (Up or Down)	Five-day Maximum Gain or Loss	Price Movement That Will Wipe Out Cash Investment
Corn (5,000 bushels)	$1.75	$ 8,750	$ 500	$.10 per bushel/ $500 per contract	$ 2,500	– $.10/ bushel
Wheat (5,000 bushels)	$2.82	$14,100	$1,000	$.20 per bushel/ $1,000 per contract	$ 5,000	– $.20/ bushel
Soybeans (5,000 bushels)	$5.31	$26,550	$1,250	$.30 per bushel/ $1,500 per contract	$ 7,500	– $.25/ bushel
Silver (5,000 troy ounces)	$7.57	$37,850	$5,000	$.50 per ounce/ $2,500 per contract	$12,500	– $1/ ounce
Gold (100 troy ounces)	$459	$45,900	$2,500	$.25 per ounce/ $2,500 per contract	$12,500	– $25/ ounce

*Required by E. F. Hutton for the small trader-speculator, as of 9/17/87

creasing population, of course, means greater demand. Each year and with each crop, it's a guess as to which of these three factors is going to be more influential.

Playing commodities is not a matter of putting your money down and walking away with the assumption your work is over. People who play commodities must check frequently on how they're doing. There are no dividends as consolation; there are only winners and losers. Since the vast majority of people involved in commodities are speculating (they're not really planning on buying crops and selling them), about half the people who play will win and half will lose. Of course, the middleman, the broker, wins every time: He or she receives a commission on every sale.

As in the stock market, the commodity market has its *fundamentalists* and its *technicians*. The technicians look at a particular commodity only in terms of the price activity of that commodity. For example, if they look at coffee in an effort to decide whether or not it's a good buy, they base their decisions on such factors as how many contracts have been sold or bought in the past month, whether the price has been going up or down during the last week or month, variations in price on days when there are a lot of contracts sold and whether the price hit a new high in the past month. Based on that information, they then decide whether or not to buy.

Technicians *don't* look at the value of the commodity; they *don't* look at things such as weather, consumer demand, medical information or new farming techniques. They assume that all this information has already been reviewed so carefully that the market has adjusted for it. They base their decisions entirely on the technical pattern of the price of the commodity, and they may adhere strictly to personal rules of thumb, for example, "Always buy when a commodity hits a new high four weeks in a row and sell if a commodity hits a new low four weeks in a row." Technicians are often called *chartists*. By charting on graph paper the past activity of the commodity, they make decisions about the future.

Fundamentalists look at the value of the commodity. They take into account the price a commodity is selling for, as well as such factors as weather, demand, population and new technology, and they make decisions about what the market price is likely to be before the contract expires. Then, based on these factors, they decide whether to buy or to sell.

Chartists, or technicians, tend to handle more trades. They buy and sell more frequently. If they buy a contract and it goes down one or two cents, they may immediately sell their contract. Fundamentalists, on the other hand, will wait out all the fluctuations in price until the commodity reaches the price they are hoping for. The fundamentalists' approach is less nerve-racking, but it does require financial staying power. The chartists who buy wheat at $2.30 a bushel and hold onto it as it goes up to $2.35 a bushel, will sell when the price drops two or three cents, whereas the fundamentalists will wait until the price goes even higher, and—if their hunches are right—will make a lot more money on the transaction than will the chartists.

Anyone who deals with commodities can find it a chancy, nerve-racking game. When prices go up people often have the courage to hold out, but when prices drop, they find it hard to wait for realization of their hoped-for appreciation. The commodity market is certainly not a field for the timid or for the long-term investor. Nevertheless, if you like to take risks, like the feeling of gambling and think you can out-forecast the other people who are predicting the future prices of commodities—be they grains, soybeans, animal products or metals—then it's a game in which you're sure to find action and perhaps some satisfaction.

Commodity Options

If you want to *play*, but feel that commodities are too risky, you might consider commodity options, which are similar to calls for stocks. Options available include silver, gold, sugar, soybeans, cattle, corn, wheat, government bonds, Swiss francs and oil.

A commodity option is the right to buy (or sell) a certain quantity of a commodity at a specific price until a specific date. These call options limit your losses, are not bought on borrowed money and allow you to sleep at night. However, if your commodity stays level—doesn't rise in price—then just as with stock calls, you would lose your investment. In contrast, if you actually bought the commodity contract and the price stayed level, you would break even.

Let's look at an example of a commodity option at work. On December 12 you could buy the right to purchase 5,000 ounces of silver at $7.50 an ounce. Purchasing this right would cost you 65 cents × 5,000 ounces, or $3,250, plus a small commission. That meant that if, before this option expired, the cash price of silver rose to, let us say $8.50, you would receive, if you chose, $1 profit less your 65-cent cost for each ounce of silver. Another way of looking at this is you could buy the silver for $7.50 on ounce and resell it immediately for $8.50 an ounce. This $5,000 proceed less your $3,250 cost less your nominal commission would represent your profit.

If, however, silver were $7.50 an ounce when your option expired, you would have made nothing from buying silver at $7.50 and selling it at $7.50, and you would have lost the investment of $3,250. Clearly, if silver were worth less than $7.50 an ounce when this option expired, your $3,250 is worth nothing. If you did well and silver, let us say, went to $12.50 an ounce, you would make $25,000 less the $3,250 cost of the call less the commission. Such a large, fast move is unlikely, however. Most buyers of calls see the calls expire at a loss.

If action is more important to you than winning or losing, then commodities may be for you. Or, if you are very knowledgeable in any of the various product areas, and you see possibilities in the market, want to take advantage of them and have the courage to withstand the risks, then this may be a place where you can make a quick profit, The reality is, however, that very few people have the knowledge or abilities to understand the national and international consequences of commodities to the extent that they will be able to take the risks with confidence. It's an area in which a few people have taken small amounts of money and turned them into very large amounts very quickly. For most, though, it's an area in which money was gambled and lost. For this reason, it's an inappropriate place to put hard-earned savings.

12

Collecting for Future Profit: Art, Stamps, Antiques, Etc.

The greatest setback you suffer is in your first minute of ownership.

Not too infrequently we read in the newspaper about someone who bought a piece of art for $500 and sold it for $20,000, or someone who bought a stamp for $3 and sold it for $300 or someone who bought an old Japanese plate for $2 at an auction and later found out that it was worth $10,000. These things do happen, but what you don't hear about are the thousands of transactions in which someone buys a commodity, i.e., an antique, a stamp or a porcelain collection, and sells it ten years later for the same price he or she paid for it—or even less. That isn't news.

All the collector investments have the same two disadvantages: lack of liquidity and the dealer's commission.

Harry Winston, the largest dealer in diamonds in the United States, admitted in a televised interview that lay investors have special difficulties in using diamonds as an investment vehicle. The biggest problem for lay investors in diamonds is that the markup from the dealer may be as high as

100 percent. Thus, if you buy a diamond for $5,000 it may have cost the dealer only $2,500. As a result, even if the diamond doubles in value in ten years' time, when you try to sell it for $10,000 you won't be able to because you are not a retailer and you can't command the prices of Harry Winston or other large jewelers. You'll wind up selling to a wholesaler who'll give you $5,000, exactly what you paid for it in the first place. In other words, because the middleman's cut is frequently as much as 50 percent of what the jewel is worth, the diamond has to double in value for you to break even.

The same can be true with antiques, art and most other collector's items that are bought or sold through collector's shops such as antique or jewelry stores. For many of these collector items, particularly the more obscure ones, the turnover is very low; for this reason the dealers must demand and get a high profit margin. If you buy directly from these dealers, the markup is included in the price you pay. The greatest setback you suffer is in your first minute of ownership. If you need to sell your precious object soon after buying it, you will suffer a significant loss. You are also subject to the whims of the marketplace: From the moment of purchase, your object will appreciate or depreciate, depending on whether or not it remains popular and in vogue.

"But," you ask, "how do the dealers get their goods in the first place?" How do they get them at half the price that you might have to pay for them? Well, part of the answer is that dealers advertise; they have feelers out in a lot of different places, always looking for good buys. They go to a lot of auctions and pick over a lot of goods. In addition, however, they have a bargaining power that you don't. They can leave things on display in their stores for a year, things they might have bought of $1,000 and priced for sale at $3,000. In one year, 10,000 people may walk by an item and one of them might want it. You, with your precious items in your living room or in a vault, don't have that marketing power.

If you are going to become a collector and are determined to invest, first and foremost you must know your field. Rather than dabbling in antiques, stamps and coins, specialize in one thing, so that when you do see a real value, you'll know it. There are, from time to time, good bargains to be had in the market. Sometimes people sell all the possessions in their home before they move and are unaware of their value as antiques. Auctions and estate sales often reward buyers with real bargains. You, being an expert in that area, will recognize the true value of the objects, buy them and sell them at a great profit. It's hard to depend on investing in this way, however, because it is impossible to predict when you're going to discover such an unrecognized treasure. Your odds are better, of course, if you make this a full-time occupation, open a store and become a dealer.

None of this is meant to indicate that there is anything wrong with becoming a collector if you enjoy collecting things. If you see it as a hobby or as a form of consumption, then you'll be getting rewards through use and enjoyment. The more involved you become in your collector's hobby, the more likely you are to succeed, because you'll get to know the field well. Over a period of time, you probably will get your money back from what you buy if you know what you're doing. Suppose you buy a diamond for $10,000 with a wholesale value of $5,000. The more rapid the inflation rate, the sooner the diamond will be worth the $10,000 you paid for it on the wholesale market and, from that point on, the sooner you'll be able to realize more dollars than you paid for your diamond.

Most investments aren't as much fun as collecting. They don't give you the pleasures of using as well as storing your wealth. If you are willing to turn this passion into a full-time occupation or if you're willing to accept it as a mediocre investment that also can be fun and pleasurable, then it may be for you.

13

Precious Metals

At its peak in 1980, gold sold for just over $850 an ounce. Seven years later, prices of goods in general were up 55 percent, but gold was selling at $400 an ounce. It is clearly not a dependable inflation hedge.

From 1971 through 1980, gold increased in price from $36 to nearly $850 an ounce, and silver increased from $1.29 to $50 an ounce. Both of these metals had recorded little increase in price for the 35 years preceding 1971, so if you had bought gold in 1940 and held it until 1970, you would have had virtually a zero rate of return on your investment. If you had bought it in 1971 and sold it in 1980, however, you clearly would have done well.

To see how the value of gold and silver is determined, we have to look at supply and demand, ornamental values and government-dictated values. Until 1971 the U.S. government cashed in U.S. dollars on demand by foreign governments and exchanged them for gold at the price of $42 an ounce. Under the Nixon administration this practice was terminated, because our gold supply was being depleted. No longer could anyone exchange currency for gold from the U.S. Treasury. Up until that time, the U.S. government's official price had put a market lid on what people around the world would pay for gold. Thereafter the price of gold began to climb slowly. With the onset of increasing inflation in 1973 and double-digit inflation in 1974—which was happening not just in the United States but around the world—some people feared that paper money would become worthless. Because of this they wanted to trade in their paper money for something they knew would always have value: gold.

For centuries, gold has been the primary token of monetary value. Paper currencies might become valueless because governments print too much currency, but gold will always maintain some value. The reasons for this are not entirely rational. Gold has some value from an industrial point of view, but not nearly as much as its value in the market. The most common industrial use for gold is in dentists' offices, but dentists have other materials available for about $5 an ounce which work almost as well. Gold's most valuable, practical use is for jewelry.

Putting practical considerations aside however, most gold that is privately owned today is hoarded and kept in the form of coins and bars, and it is held by people who have exchanged their currency for gold. When gold rose from $42 to $850 an ounce, it wasn't because currency had fallen in value proportionately. It hadn't. Rather, people were buying gold out of panic, brought on by a fear that inflation would not remain at a 12 percent rate but might accelerate to 50 or 100 percent. Some people remembered Germany in the early 1920s, when a loaf of bread cost one million marks and people had to shop with wheelbarrows full of money. People thought that if you bought $100 worth of gold and the $100 would buy a month's supply of groceries, no matter what happened to prices, that same amount of gold would always take care of the groceries for one month.

The price of silver also has risen, tending to move in tandem with gold. When people are looking for a precious metal to hoard as a means of preserving wealth, silver is also popular.

Silver's value is based on a more rational market than the market for gold, primarily because silver has substantial industrial as well as ornamental use. Until 1975 it was illegal for U.S. citizens to buy gold in any form other than precious gold coins. However, there were none of the same rules against owning silver. Silver could be bought in any form, including what were called *junk bags* of quarters. Until 1964 all quarters contained 90 percent silver, but in 1965 the U.S. Mint stopped putting silver in quarters. In 1987 a bag of quarters with a face value of $1,000, dated 1964 or earlier, was selling for approximately $5,300 because of its silver content. These bags were popular as a savings device. People who see an economic doomsday coming can buy a $1,000 bag of quarters and feel that when the envisioned day comes and paper money is worthless, they can take their silver quarters to the store and buy groceries or other necessities with them.

Gold and Silver You Can Hold

If you want to own gold so that you can hold it in your hand and touch it, the most common and practical way is by buying U.S. American Eagle coins. These coins are pure gold and have face values of $50, $25, $10 and $5. The $50 coin contains one pure ounce of gold and the $5 coin contains 1/10 of an ounce. They can be purchased through dealers, coin stores and some banks and they sell at a premium. Typically, you pay five percent to seven percent over the present market value of the gold content. Recently, with gold trading at $460 an ounce, I called a broker to get a quote and found I could buy the one-ounce American Eagle for $495. If I had wanted to sell the coin through the same dealer, he would buy it for $460. The premiums are larger for the smaller denominations. One advantage of the smaller coins, however, is that they can be used as jewelry at the same time as a store value.

A second choice that was popular before the American Eagle was introduced was the South African Krugerrand. The premium is smaller, but often you have to sell the Krugerrand at a discount below actual gold content value.

The simplest way to buy silver, along with junk bags, is the silver Eagle. This American coin has a face value of $1 and contains one troy ounce of silver. Again, you pay a premium above the silver content value. A dealer told me recently that a silver Eagle would cost me $11; silver was selling at $7.60 an ounce. If I wanted to sell one silver Eagle, the dealer would pay $8. Of course, the larger the volume I wanted to buy or sell, the better the price I would receive.

When in the market for buying silver through coins or junk bags or buying gold through coins, it is best to check several dealers and banks in your area. Some banks do offer these American gold and silver coins, sometimes at better and often at worse prices than coin dealers.

Keep in mind buying gold and silver is similar to investing in collectibles. You pay a premium to buy and, if you turn around and sell immediately, you will lose money. You need a certain rise in the market value of gold and silver just to break even. While you hold these coins they bring no income, but should their values soar, you'll also have the satisfaction of knowing they're in your drawer or on your necklace.

For the speculator and gambler, options as well as low margin contracts are also available for gold and silver on the Chicago Board of Trade (see Table 11.1).

In my opinion, buying metals is an appropriate investment only for the very wealthy, and then only if it is viewed as a doomsday investment. If you have $1 million and want to make sure you'll never go hungry in the event of a total economic catastrophe, it would not be unwise for you to put $20,000 or $30,000 into precious metals. Keep in mind, however, that the purchase of metals should be considered only a defensive or protective investment; it is not a reliable way to accumulate wealth.

Mining Stocks

Another way to invest in the future of precious metals is to buy mining stocks. You can buy mining stocks of South African gold companies; they pay substantial yields. These gold mines, however, are depleting resources that may last anywhere from three to 30 years, and then all the dividends and earnings will stop. You always run the risk of price fluctuations in gold, but at the moment the biggest risk in these mining stock investments is based on politics. In South Africa, for example, the possibility of revolution is always imminent. In a revolution—one that's successful, anyway—there's a chance that the new government will confiscate the gold mines and convert them to state ownership, giving your stock a value of zero.

Some U.S. mining stocks tend to sell at high multipliers and pay a very low dividend ranging from one to three percent. These stocks tend to move up when the stock market moves down, although there is no guarantee this will happen. During the market plunge from 1971 to 1974, mining stocks were the only ones that consistently moved up. They moved up because the price of gold and silver had increased. In 1987, however, an exception to this occurred, as gold and stocks soared.

Platinum

A third and much less actively-traded precious metal is platinum. Unlike gold with its basic use as a store value and jewelry, platinum has increasing industrial use. It is used in catalytic converters and in computers and circuitry. There are very few platinum-producing mines. Most people buying contracts in platinum are users, whereas with gold and silver the majority of buyers are speculators and investors. The cost of platinum is much closer to that of gold than silver. At this writing, platinum is approximately $600 an ounce. Historically, it has traded at $100 to $150 an ounce more than gold, but there have been periods when the price of platinum has dipped below the price of gold. There is no special reason to assume that formula will continue in the future, but many speculators claim that when the price of platinum dips below the price of gold, an opportunity in platinum exists.

Investments in platinum can be made the same as in other precious metals, including investing in the metal itself and in mining stocks of companies that mine platinum. However, there are fewer such mining stocks and the market for speculating in platinum is much less liquid than those for gold or silver. Fluctuations in the value of platinum are related more to supply and demand for its use in industry and less to fears of inflation. Therefore, if you are using precious metals as a hedge against inflation, silver and gold are better choices. Investing successfully in platinum requires gaining a special knowledge of today's technologies and the metal's applications and an understanding of how both affect market forces and prices.

If you do want to *play* metals, their stocks are a better bet than the metals themselves. They produce income, are liquid and will move with the price of precious metals.

For 99 percent of Americans, investing directly in precious metals is inappropriate. You earn no income while you are holding the metals and you have no guarantee that they are going to increase even if inflation accelerates (see Figure 13.1). At its peak in 1980, gold sold for just over $850 an ounce. Seven years later, prices of goods in general were up 55 percent, but gold was selling at $400 an ounce. It is clearly not a dependable inflation hedge. The silver story is just the same.

If you want a hedge against inflation, an income-producing piece of real estate will better serve this end. As prices rise, so do rents and values of income properties. Finally, there is no logical, absolute guarantee that inflation will cause metals to go up. But when inflation occurs and prices of commodities or services and labor rise, apartment buildings go up in price because the costs of constructing them go up. That pushes the value of existing apartment buildings even higher. It's hard to find a good rationale for the small investor to be involved in precious metals.

FIGURE 13.1   Cost of Living

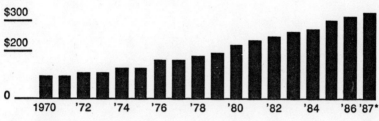

What it takes to buy what 100 dollars bought in 1970.

*August 1987

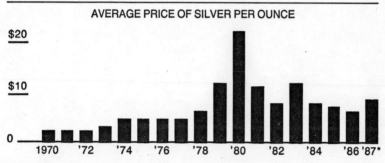

AVERAGE PRICE OF SILVER PER OUNCE

*September 1987

AVERAGE PRICE OF GOLD PER OUNCE

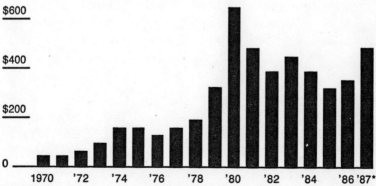

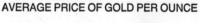

*September 1987

14

Tax Shelters and Write-Offs

It's hard enough to assess the value of a two-flat a mile from your home. It's just too hard to assess the future of a herd of cattle in Texas if you live in a Boston high rise.

The 1986 Tax Reform Act (TRA) did much to reduce the attractiveness of tax shelters to investors. First, since the highest tax brackets were reduced substantially, tax shelters no longer provide as much benefit. If, let us say, in 1985 a tax shelter generated a write-off from ordinary income of $10,000, and you were in a 50 percent tax bracket, the shelter would save you $5,000. Under the new law, it may generate the same write-off, but only save you 28 percent of your taxable income, or $2,800. In addition, the 1986 TRA disallowed the investor in a limited partnership to write off loses of that partnership against ordinary income. Starting in 1987, investors would only be able to write off such income against other passive investments. This is being phased in, so that in 1988 you still receive 40 percent of the previous benefits, but by 1991, there will be no tax write-off against personal income.

There are, however, two major areas that are still available for tax shelter investments: direct or general partnership investments in real estate, and oil and gas drilling partnerships.

Real Estate Tax Shelters

Your home and your second home still remain to some extent tax shelters. You can still write off your mortgage interest and real estate taxes against your ordinary income. The direct purchase of investment real estate also remains a potential tax shelter. You may write off up to $25,000 of your losses from operating real estate against your ordinary income. However, if you earn over $100,000, this benefit was reduced, and if you earn over $150,000, you cannot write off any real estate losses against your ordinary income.

The real estate limited partnership remains a vehicle for cash flow and appreciation, but the very popular partnership built around a tax shelter as the main selling tool is all but dead.

A general partnership remains a possible tax shelter. There may be a managing partner who finds an investment and brings in five to ten investors such as yourself. You must be as liable on the mortgage as is the general partner. If the mortgage is from a financial institution, personal liability is not required by the IRS, but if the mortgage is from an individual who sold the building to your partnership, you all must be liable for that mortgage. To get a write-off against ordinary income, you also must be active in the management of the property. You must have some say in the rents, repairs and management of the building on a regular basis. Even if you own an income property yourself, in theory the IRS would not let you write off losses against ordinary income if you have nothing at all to do with its operations, i.e., if you live in Florida, the property is in New York, and you simply receive monthly checks from a property management company and speak with them a few times a year.

The IRS is mainly concerned about the wealthy investors who were getting big tax write-offs with no involvement in the properties. While the law reads that to get write-offs you must be active on a regular basis in the management of the property, I think it's unlikely they'll come after people who own the properties themselves, but who are not at all active in the management.

There are a couple exceptions to the elimination of limited partnerships as tax shelters. To encourage historic renovation and construction of low-income housing, the IRS has made an exception. You can be a limited partner in a partnership that restores historic buildings and get up to a $25,000 tax credit. You don't have to participate actively in the project and you can be a limited partner. This maximum $25,000 credit is not a write-off against ordinary income; rather, it is a $25,000 reduction in your tax bill. The credit is based on 20 percent of the rehabilitation dollars that go into a historic structure. There are lesser such credits allowed for buildings that aren't certified as historic, and these credits can still be quite valuable.

The law also creates tax credits for investment in low-income housing. Here the same $25,000 maximum credit is achievable. If the partnership builds or rehabilitates a building for low-income units, nine percent of its expenses are direct tax credits for the first ten years of operation (if not financed with tax-exempt bonds or federal subsidies). If the project is subsidized or was merely acquired rather than built or rehabilitated, an annual credit of four percent of expenses applies.

The simplest real estate tax shelter is your home. Perhaps the most profitable is directly purchasing investment property, but that requires work, time and some risk. An active partnership may work for you, but make sure that you do in fact have a role in the partnership that you can document for the IRS. The limited partnerships in historic renovation and low-income housing may also be worth looking into, but make sure you have the sales prospectus checked by your accountant and also, if possible, by someone who understands the real estate market involved.

Oil and Gas Drilling

Oil and gas drilling partnerships were spared by the Tax Reform Act of 1986. Before 1986 these limited partnerships provided substantial tax write-offs. Today these write-offs are available if you have a *working interest* in a partnership for oil and gas. A working interest means you are liable for partnership liabilities and you could possibly face additional financial exposure if problems develop. You must be at risk. You must also have some voice in making decisions should they be necessary. Basically, you still are a passive investor, but you are on the hook if there is trouble, and you have a vote in operations when major decisions are to be made.

One of the problems of investing in these partnerships is the difficulty of assessing the value. It's hard enough to assess the value of a partnership in real estate in another city or in several buildings, but it is much more difficult to assess the likelihood of striking oil. Most people who will expose you to these partnerships are salespeople who will make a large commission if you buy. Unless your accountant or financial advisor has a track record with the partnership and can fully recommend it, I would discourage you from putting your money into something that is so hard to assess intelligently.

Other Tax Write-Offs

Other tax write-off schemes, I'm sure, will be offered by syndicators. I'd be very leery of any of the *exotics*, be they cattle, plane leasing or alligator farming. It's hard enough to assess the value of a two-flat a mile from your home. It's just too hard to assess the future of a herd of cattle in Texas if you live in a Boston high rise.

The Simplest Tax Shelter

Municipal bonds represent the simplest of all tax shelters. In most states when you buy a municipal bond the interest is not taxable in your state or by the federal government. Most are safe and liquid and carry a very low commission rate to buy and sell and no management hassles. While they do represent the lowest rate of return, they also represent the highest degree of safety and liquidity.

15

Retirement Investing: IRAs, Keoghs...

All these investment vehicles have one characteristic in common, and the best of them share a second characteristic as well.

There is a dizzying array of retirement investments, including IRAs, Keoghs, SEPs, 403(b)s, single premium life insurance and tax-deferred annuities. All these investment vehicles have one characteristic in common, and the best of them share a second characteristic as well. All retirement accounts allow the investor to set aside a specified number of dollars that will grow, tax deferred, until retirement. In other words, the money put aside today can earn dividends, interest and capital gains, compound those dollars, and the earnings are exempt from state and federal taxes while they accumulate, until at retirement when those dollars are taxed only as they are withdrawn from the retirement investment account. Tax deferral makes these investments attractive. What makes them almost irresistible is when a second benefit is added. Many retirement investments allow you to subtract the amounts invested from your taxable income. This means that if you set aside $1,000 and are in a 28 percent income bracket, you would save $280 that year in income taxes.

Which Retirement Accounts Are for Me?

The best of all retirement accounts include both the above benefits: Money accumulates tax deferred until retirement, and you get an immediate tax write-off for setting those dollars aside. This double benefit is available in Keogh accounts, 401(k)s, SEPs, 403(b)s and IRAs, at least for most of us. There are numerous retirement investments. I will not discuss all of them, but will discuss those that apply to most of us.

IRAs

In 1982 Congress passed legislation that changed the form of retirement investing in the United States: Individual Retirement Accounts—IRAs—were introduced. IRAs allow an individual to set aside $2,000 each year into a specified IRA account. A married couple in which one works can set aside $2,250 and a two-career married couple can set aside up to $4,000 between them. This can be done regardless of how much money you earn. Of course, if you earn $1,000 and set aside $2,000 in your IRA, you won't get much of a tax break on that year's earnings.

Investing in an IRA offers many benefits. Not only can you accumulate this money, tax deferred, until age 59½, but if you qualify, the $2,000 can be a write-off against present income as well. If a single individual earning over $17,800 takes a $2,000 IRA deduction and deposits $2,000 in an IRA account, he or she reduces present income taxes by $560 and also can build up that $2,000 tax deferred until age 59½ or older. Again, for a married couple, the maximums are $2,250 if one works and $4,000 if both work. You don't have to set aside these entire amounts; these are the maximums allowed. You can set aside whatever part of it you're comfortable with.

A Convincing Case for IRAs

Let's examine the power of the double effect of not having to pay tax on the $2,000 and also allowing it to earn income, tax free, until retirement. Let's compare $2,000 deposited in your own bank account with no IRA benefits, and $2,000 set aside in an IRA. Let's assume you're 30 years old, and compare the gains you'll have made when you reach age 60 with these two alternatives.

The difference is substantial. To begin, your non-IRA retirement fund started with only $1,440 out of the original $2,000 because you had to pay 28 percent to the government in taxes. In addition, every dollar of your savings account interest is taxable; therefore, assuming you earn ten percent pretax on the investment, you'd only earn 7.2 percent after-tax on the nonsheltered retirement investment. The result is that at age 60 your IRA account would have increased from $2,000 to $34,898 due to compound interest, while your bank account would contain $13,706 because you had to pay income tax all that time without the benefit of any tax write-offs or with no deferrals.

Despite the fact that your withdrawals are subject to income taxes as the money is withdrawn from the IRA account, the advantages still far outweigh those of the other version, where you paid Uncle Sam as you went along.

What Are the Restrictions of an IRA?

An IRA must be set up by April 15 for the preceding year's taxable income. If you're filing your 1988 tax return, you must set up the IRA by April 15, 1989, to get the deductions. In other words, you can do it at the last minute. The IRS must approve the trustee holding the IRA, but approved trustees include almost all banks, savings and loans, stock-brokerage firms, mutual fund management companies and many others. If in doubt, ask to see their IRS approval letter.

The money can be invested in almost any investment vehicle, excluding life insurance and collectibles such as art, diamonds, gold and silver. You can even invest in U.S.-minted gold and silver coins.

Who Is Not Eligible for an IRA?

If you don't file an income tax return or if you have no compensation, you are not eligible. Therefore, almost any working individual is eligible.

Unfortunately, many people are not eligible for the tax write-off aspect of the IRA: If you, as an individual, earn $35,000, or as a married couple, $50,000, and one or both of you are covered by a retirement plan at work, you are not eligible for the immediate tax write-off of an IRA. However, you can still set up an IRA and get the tax-deferral benefits until retirement. If you, as an individual, earn less than $25,000 or as a married couple less than $40,000, you are fully eligible for both benefits. When your income is in between, your eligibility for the write-off is proportional to your income. For example, if as a married couple you earn $45,000, you can get half the write-off for your $2,000 IRA contribution, or a $1,000 write-off.

If, let us say, as a couple you earn $45,000 before any retirement investing, and at work, $5,000 of one or both of your incomes were set aside into an appropriate retirement or pension account, you then are fully eligible for the IRA write-off because you now have $40,000 in taxable income.

For those who qualify for both benefits, IRAs are hard to beat. They are simple and low cost to set up and you have control over where the money is invested.

401(k)s

Ninety percent of U.S. corporations are covered by 401(k)s, through which your employer takes up to $7,000 or 20 percent of your income, whichever is less, and puts it in a retirement account. Your employer may match part or all of your contribution with its own dollars. Keep in mind you can have both an IRA and a 401(k). The benefits are the same as described above for an IRA, only the dollar amounts are different.

Keoghs: Who Is Eligible and How Do They Work?

Keogh retirement plans are available to individuals who own their own businesses—professionals such as attorneys and doctors, or small business owners. Keoghs are available to sole proprietorships or partnerships, but not to corporations.

Keoghs have one big advantage over IRAs: The amount allowed is much larger. You can invest up to $30,000 or 20 percent of your income, whichever is less. Keogh funds are handled basically the same as IRAs, with some small differences. One is that you much establish your Keogh account by December 31 of the year in which you plan to apply it, rather than $3^{1}/_2$ months later with an IRA.

SEPs and 403(b)s

Retirement accounts called *403(b)s* are similar to 401(k)s. The primary difference is that 403(b)s are available to government employees, public teachers and some nonprofit institutional employees. SEPs—Simplified Employee Pension Plans—require less bookkeeping than 401(k)s and offer higher dollar amounts, i.e., up to $30,000 or 25 percent of income, whichever is less. They can be set up only by the employer and the employer must fund these accounts for all employees.

Some Common Costs of Retirement Investments

All these investments have in common a penalty for early withdrawal. You not only pay the deferred income tax on the money withdrawn if you withdraw it before age $59^{1}/_2$, but you also pay a ten percent penalty on the money withdrawn. You can allow the money to accumulate, tax deferred, until age $70^{1}/_2$, but then must withdraw the money so that is all gone by the time the government expects you to die. For example, if at age 70 your life expectancy is fourteen more years, you must make fourteen yearly withdrawals that will deplete your account to zero. If not, you will be penalized.

Keep in mind that these accounts are tax deferred, *not* tax free. As you withdraw money after age 59½, it is taxed as normal income.

There are variations, but they are minor to this basic concept. You are getting a tax write-off and you are accumulating your wealth tax deferred in all of these vehicles.

Clearly your first available dollars should go into those accounts that have both tax write-off and tax-deferral benefits. If you have dollars left, consider putting them in those retirement investments that only have the tax-deferral benefit.

Single Premium or Whole Life Insurance

For those who have invested the maximum allowable dollars in the *double bang* retirement investments, single premium or whole life life insurance and tax-deferred annuities are worth looking at. With single premium policies, you pay a single premium and then for a period of ten, 20, 30 or more years, you are covered with a death benefit so that your beneficiary receives that amount should you die. In addition, you are guaranteed a certain minimum return on the money you invested. That money will be paid either as an annuity or as a lump sum upon retirement. The government allows this money to accumulate tax deferred because it is, in part, life insurance, although this represents a small part of the investment dollars of the policy. These policies provide two obvious benefits: You are covered for some life insurance benefit to your heirs and you are building a tax-deferred retirement account.

Another excellent benefit that does not apply to the previously discussed retirement account is that you can borrow against your single premium life insurance. Typically, you can borrow as much as 90 percent and you do not pay any interest out of your pocket. In most cases, you just do not earn money on that 90 percent while it's borrowed, or you pay a low interest rate. If you never pay the money back to the insurance company, that money comes out of your heirs' benefits.

There are, however, costs to what appears to be the perfect plan. There are up-front charges to the insurance company salespeople that could range anywhere from seven percent to 11 percent. The insurance companies also charge in the area of two percent a year to manage that money. With an IRA there are usually no up-front costs and minimal or no management fees, and you can put the money in a corporate bond fund and earn ten percent just like an insurance company might do, without being charged two percent for that service.

Tax-Deferred Annuities

An annuity is an ongoing stream of income for the rest of your life. A tax-deferred annuity is very similar to single premium life insurance. It lacks one benefit: There is no life insurance. A tax-deferred annuity is also different in that instead of a lump sum at retirement age, you receive a monthly income for the rest of your life. The principle is similar: You give the insurance company a lump sum of money, be it $5,000, $10,000, $100,000 or whatever. After a designated period of time, you get the benefits of that money having grown, tax deferred.

For example, let us say you are 40 years old and are planning for your retirement at age 65. You accept a proposition from a life insurance salesperson to whom you give $20,000 in cash. At age 65, that insurance company will guarantee you a monthly income for the rest of your life. This income will be based on what's in that annuity fund after 25 years of compounding its earnings. This income stream, from 65 years old until death, is called an annuity.

You can fund an annuity with any amount of money; there are no tax limitations here. In addition, you can choose whether the insurance company invests in real estate, common stocks (through mutual funds), or interest-yielding investments such as corporate or government bonds. The advantage to choosing interest-bearing investments is that you can know exactly how much you will get in income at age 65. The disadvantage is that if there is a period of high inflation, you'll wish you had invested in real estate or stocks so that you had maintained the purchasing power of your money at retirement. Fixed-income investments are great in periods of moderate or low inflation and poor in periods of very high inflation.

You can also receive a lump sum payment at age 65. This option would require you to pay a substantial tax all at once and then decide how to invest the funds. (This really shouldn't be called an annuity, but investment parlance is confusing on this point.) Also, keep in mind that there are fees similar to those with single premium life insurance.

Looking at single premium insurance and annuities is a good idea for people who want to combine retirement investing with life insurance and for people who have exhausted the retirement investments with the double benefits discussed above. Unlike the other vehicles, there is no limit to what you can invest, and you can borrow against them.

Where to Invest Retirement Account Dollars

Even though all these retirement investment vehicles offer substantial tax benefits, they are of little use if, once set up and established, the dollars are invested in vehicles that lose money. There are appropriate and inappropriate investments for retirement accounts. Since they have the benefit of tax deferral, one should never invest in municipal bonds. You can own those tax free in your own personal investment accounts. Corporate and government bonds make excellent sense for these accounts.

Zero coupon bonds fit IRAs and Keoghs like a glove. You are insured that your bond earns today's rate of interest for 20 to 30 years, but in addition, that the interest is also reinvested at the same high rate. Should rates fall in the future, you avoid the pitfall of conventional bonds: That interest earned would be reinvested at much lower rates. You know exactly what

TABLE 15.1   Future Value of One $2,000 IRA Invested at Various Interest Rates and Maturities In a Zero Coupon Bond

Maturity	Interest Rates				
	5%	8%	10%	12%	15%
10 years	$ 3,258	$ 4,318	$ 5,188	$ 6,212	$ 8,092
20 years	5,306	9,322	13,456	19,292	32,740
30 years	8,644	20,120	34,900	59,920	132,420
40 years	14,080	43,440	90,600	186,100	535,800

(For example, if you invest $2,000 in a zero coupon bond maturing in 20 years at 10% interest, you will have $13,456 coming, a bond maturing in 40 years $90,600.)

TABLE 15.2   Value of an IRA with Yearly $2,000 Deposits at Various Interest Rates and for Different Lengths of Time

Years of investing $2,000	Interest Rates				
	5%	8%	10%	12%	15%
10	$26,414	$31,290	$35,062	$ 39,310	$ 46,698
20	69,438	98,846	126,004	161,398	235,620
30	139,522	244,692	361,886	540,586	999,914
40	253,680	559,562	973,704	1,718,284	5,476,956

you'll get at maturity. Keep in mind the true historic rate of three percent interest and remember that as long as interest minus inflation is substantially higher than three percent, zero coupon bonds appear very well suited for IRAs and Keoghs. Table 15.1 illustrates the rewards of one $2,000 investment in an IRA when interest rates are high. Table 15.2 further demonstrates the impressive dollar accumulation from annual $2,000 IRA investments.

Most important of all, understand that the best investments are the ones that give you tax write-offs now and tax deferral as well. Only invest in the others if you have exhausted the opportunity to invest in these.

16

Stocks, Bonds and Real Estate: Which is Best?

Keep in mind that this formula may lead you to buy the least popular investment of the moment. That's probably a sign that it will work.

Stocks, bonds and real estate represent the three main vehicles for building retirement funds or wealth or both, whether for IRAs or personal wealth-building programs. One of these three is almost always the best investment opportunity. The problem is, *the one that's best keeps changing.*

Real Estate vs. Stock

When I wrote *Planting Your Money Tree* in 1977, I suggested buying a house soon rather than waiting, because I believed real estate prices were going to continue to rise. Well, I was right for a while. However, by 1980, the cost of homes was far outstripping people's ability to support the monthly payments on new homes and I sensed the bubble was about to burst. Stocks, on the other hand, had done poorly compared to real estate during the 1970s and were certainly out of favor. Luckily for me, I looked at both my real estate and my stocks and decided it was time to make some switches.

Most people who had money to invest at that time would have put it in real estate, in whatever form was available, rather than in stocks. They would have looked at the performance of the 1970s and seen that the real estate rate of return was much higher due to rapidly rising prices. They would have been very sorry if they'd acted on this observation. Real estate prices in general leveled off and lots of real estate even went down in price. Stocks boomed.

When I examined my own real estate income property in 1980 and looked at prices people were willing to pay for income properties, my common sense told me to sell. I sold some of it and reinvested in common stocks because I thought that was then the best opportunity. Why? Partly because it went against the common wisdom. But more than this, the numbers spoke for themselves.

Although there is no national real estate exchange to tell you prices of income-producing real estate, my experience in 1980 was that a typical newer apartment building, with the landlord paying heat and the tenants electricity, was selling at a multiplier of about seven times gross rents. In other words, if the tenants' rents totaled $10,000 per year, the building would sell for about $70,000. It's typical that in such a building about 45 percent of the rent goes toward expenses such as heat, maintenance and taxes, leaving the landlord with 55 percent or, in the case of this example, $5,500. Divide this income by the $70,000 purchase price and you get a rate of return of just under eight percent. In the early 1970s, multipliers were closer to 5.75. In other words, a building with the same income would have sold for about $58,000, or a rate of return close to ten percent.

Although there also is no one national index of all common stocks, and there was variance between over-the-counter stocks and the New York Stock Exchange, in 1980 stocks were selling at an average multiplier of 5.5 to six times net income, meaning that if a company earned $1 per share, the stock would sell on average for $5.50 or $6 per share. This means that your yield on your investment (divide one by the multiplier), whether you got it in dividends or by the company reinvesting your profits, was about 16 percent—double the yield on real estate. There also were stocks in many companies selling at three or four times earnings and therefore earning 25 percent to 33 percent returns.

Stocks also have the advantage of being comparatively liquid and a lot less grief to own. It seemed silly to hold on to apartment buildings with their inherent headaches and risks and earn an eight percent return when it was possible to earn 20 percent to 30 percent through common stocks.

This was not a popular point of view, however. When I suggested to people the time was ripe to sell real estate and reinvest in stocks, their general reaction was disbelief; it seemed so clear that real estate, and not stocks, was the place to be. Their reactions confirmed my insight: People had lost their compasses. Even though these 1980 numbers pointed toward selling real estate, I still felt queasy as I sold. Part of me (my gut) couldn't stand selling something that had kept rising in the past. It's hard to go against the accepted wisdom and sell a past winner.

A Tool to Help

I suggest that if you are deciding between investing funds in real estate or common stocks, use this tool to help you get some perspective: Look at apartment buildings or office buildings or whatever other investment real estate vehicle you are comfortable with and that is available in your community. Then divide the net income before mortgage payments by the purchase price, which will give you your investment yield if you paid all cash for the building. Compare that to the type of stocks you're comfortable investing in. To figure out that yield, divide one by the price-earnings ratio of those stocks. If the price-earnings ratio is ten, one over ten equals a ten percent earnings yield. If the gap is great between the yield on the real estate and the earnings yield on the stock, you should move your money toward the one with the much higher return.

Another way to look at this is to compare multipliers. If a stock sells at four times earnings, compare it to the multiplier on a building. For example, if a building generates rents of $10,000 and nets $5,000 after all operating expenses, it would have to sell at four times net earnings to be as attractive as a four-times-earnings stock (four times $5,000, or $20,000). This would represent a multiplier of two times gross rents. We are assuming in this example that the futures of the stock and of the building are equally rosy or gloomy.

Typically, only slum real estate or run-down rooming houses sell at such cheap prices (multipliers). But this shows how cheap stocks were in 1980. Stocks were inappropriately selling at *slum* prices.

What About Bonds?

What might warn you that a particular time is a bad time to put your money into bonds as compared to stocks or real estate? Subtracting the present inflation rate from the interest rate on bonds is one such guideline. If you get a net return of less than three percent, the bonds are yielding historically low interest. If your return is much higher than three percent, their return is atypically high. With yields on bonds at this writing at about ten percent and inflation at four percent, bonds look attractive. Unless you believe inflation is going to heat up and we're going to see hyperinflation, buying bonds, particularly zero coupon bonds for your IRA or Keogh plan, appears to be an excellent option.

At this writing in the summer of 1987, returns on common stocks are much smaller than those on real estate. By this I mean that if you looked at the P/E ratio or multiplier of common stocks, currently approximately 18, it tells us that for $1 of earnings, you pay $18. Again, based on present earnings, you'd get a return of $5^{1}/_{2}$ percent ($^{1}/_{18}$). This assumes that the company's earnings are stable and that you are in the position of full ownership of that company, i.e., what they don't pay out in dividends goes into your bank account. Currently, apartment complexes are selling at the lowest multiplier of the past 15 years. Because of the Tax Reform Act of 1986 they have lost a lot of their appeal. I estimate the average multiplier for apartment complexes is running at approximately $5^1/4$ times gross rent, down from seven times rent in the early 1980s. This means that, after all expenses, you can buy apartment complexes at about ten times the net income. So while stocks are yielding a $5^1/2$ percent return on investment, based on present earnings, real estate is yielding approximately a ten percent return. Real estate investing is not popular or hot, so at this juncture it appears that investing in an apartment building, for the long haul, is a better bet than putting your money in common stocks.

The hope is if you invest in an apartment building or other income-producing real estate at some time in the future, real estate again will become a hot investment vehicle, your real estate will sell at a much higher price than you paid, and it will be time to consider cashing in your chips and moving on.

Bonds vs. Stocks or Real Estate

Once you have determined whether to buy stocks or real estate, how do you compare that better investment—in this case real estate—to the attractiveness of bonds? In order to compare oranges to oranges, you need to compare the absolute rate of return on bonds with that of the better of stocks or real estate.

As we have seen, real estate and bonds are earning approximately the same: Ten percent. When the rates are that close together, it is not a clear-cut decision. Bonds offer the certainty of knowing what you'll earn as well as liquidity and much less grief in ownership. Real estate offers the possibility of capital gains, an inflation hedge and leverage.

If you're very close to retirement age, equity investments such as stocks and real estate become less appropriate and specific interest-bearing investments more appropriate. But for those of you who have a long time before retirement and are deciding in which vehicle to invest, I suggest the following method. Compare:

1. Rate of return on bonds (without considering inflation);
2. Rate of return on stocks (one divided by the price-earnings ratio); and
3. Rate of return on real estate (net operating income before mortgage payment divided by purchase price).

See which is highest. If all three are close, buy bonds for the certainty of income and peace of mind, particularly for IRAs. If one rate of return—be it bonds, real estate or stocks—is way above the rest, go with that one. Keep in mind that this formula may lead you to buy the least popular investment of the moment. That's probably a sign that it will work.

17

Your Overall Investment Strategy

Over the long haul, it's clear that equity investments—common stocks and real estate—are a much better vehicle for building wealth for the average small investor than anything else available.

Where you put your savings has a lot to do with who you are, what you've got and what you want.

If you're 65 years old and have a net worth of $500,000, you'll want to maximize your present income as well as diversify your holdings. At this stage in life it's very difficult to start over again if you make a colossal mistake. You're at an age where you want to enjoy what you've earned. Therefore, you should convert your assets to high-yielding investments, which will allow you to enjoy a good income during your remaining years. Investing in small businesses is too much work; buying real estate requires more hard work than you may desire; but if you already own some real estate that has a substantial cash flow and can afford to pay for professional management, you may want to consider holding on to some of that real estate. You may want to distribute the remainder of your funds in bonds, high-yield common stocks and cash. For your own peace of mind you may want to invest $10,000 or $20,000 in precious metals. Safety, income, liquidity and lack of need for personal management should dominate your decisions at this point in life.

If you are 30 years old, have a good job and $15,000 to invest, you might do well to have an entirely different outlook on investing than a person approaching retirement. You can afford more risks and are probably going to be more active in the supervision of your investments. Over the long haul, it's clear that equity investments—common stocks and real estate—are a much better vehicle for building wealth for the average small investor than anything else available. Bonds, historically, have not reaped great rewards over the long haul. There are, however, moments of opportunity even in bonds. When the true rate of return (interest rate minus inflation rate) is historically high. This opportunity should not be ignored. However, keep in mind that over the long haul, wealth is made more often in real estate than any other vehicle and that if you carefully pursue that endeavor, or find undiscovered growth stocks, you'll be adding your own energies to influencing your outcome.

When you're older the key is diversity; when you're young the key is to put most of your eggs in one basket—but watch that basket very carefully. Common stocks can be a vehicle to accumulating wealth if you buy stocks, as described earlier, in small growing companies that are undervalued by the market. This course doesn't have to involve extreme risk, because selecting undervalued stocks means selecting stocks with very little downside risk. Another advantage of this route is that once you have selected the stocks, you needn't spend a good deal of time managing your investment. It's a liquid investment; you can sell it and get your money within five days from your stockbroker. If you invest $12,000 of your $15,000 in common stocks, you shouldn't buy stocks in more than two or three companies. Buying stocks in six or eight companies with such an amount of money insures that even if one stock goes up six or sevenfold, your overall portfolio won't show a huge increase. Therefore, pick only the few that look best to you.

Again, if you are young, another route most likely to create wealth for you is real estate, but there are disadvantages here. These investments require patience, initiative and substantial debt. Another disadvantage is that real estate is not a liquid investment. If you decide you want to sell, it may take six months or one year before you receive your cash. However, instances of people who started with modest funds and built substantial wealth and income from real estate are much more frequent than they are in the stock market. More people have become well-to-do through real estate than through any other vehicle, including small businesses, retailing, franchising or the stock market—and income property represents your best inflation hedge.

Another route to wealth is owning a small business or a franchise—if you have a lot of energy, ambition and are interested in running a business. Starting your own business may not require a huge amount of capital, but it does take a huge amount of energy, ability and creativity.

IRAs, Keoghs and the rest should be part of almost everybody's investment planning. If you're under 59, you're foolish not to be taking advantage of all the benefits I've discussed.

I have described two categories of people at different extremes of investment needs and goals. It's up to you to decide where you fit between these two. Only you know your willingness to take risks, your need for liquidity and your amount of free time and energy.

Good Luck!

APPENDIX

Resources: The Cream of the Crop

There are literally thousands of information resources for the various investments discussed in this book. Rather than give you an exhaustive list of several hundred financial resources, I'll share with you the cream of the crop: the books, magazines and newsletters I find continually useful in staying on course in my own investing.

The Wall Street Journal, day after day and year after year, remains the most important of all financial resources. Read it daily to keep abreast of financial trends. It's not crucial to read it cover to cover, but certainly read the front page and the earnings reports and browse through it for articles of interest to you.

The *USA Today* business section is brief, to the point, and often has very worthwhile articles.

Another excellent resource is *Barron's*, which is sort of a Saturday *Wall Street Journal*. *Barron's* has a knack for knocking the wind out of the sails of overpriced markets and alerting you to bargains that prevail due to doom and gloom psychology. An advantage of reading *Barron's* is that it offers many short-term sample subscriptions to different financial information resources.

I've read *Forbes* for years. It's an excellent financial review, with many articles that point out changing financial trends and opportunities before the ideas are popular. Of particular interest are the columns in the back of the magazine every week, written by investment advisors who think for themselves and can see the forest for the trees.

Currently there are hundreds of newsletters. One, *Mark Hulbert's Financial Digest*, even ranks the effectiveness of newsletters. Three or four newsletters are particularly good. At the top of the list is *Al Frank's Prudent Speculator*. The criteria he uses to evaluate companies are similar to those suggested in my book. Frank looks for companies that are undervalued in terms of sales per share, earnings per share and assets per share. Incidentally, Hulbert's rating shows the *Prudent Speculator* had the most successful track record of all newsletters from 1981 through 1987. According to Hulbert, following Frank's advice would have yielded approximately a 700 percent return during this period. I like the *Prudent Speculator* not just for the spectacular results, but because I believe his results are based on sound investment principles. Sometimes newsletters can brag about results for a one- or two-year period, but often those shorter-term results are a matter of luck.

I also recommend the *Value Line Service*, which reviews 1,700 stocks in-depth, and the Value Line Convertible service which reviews convertible bonds and convertible preferred stocks. Frequently *Barron's* contains offerings for the Value Line newsletter service which allow you to sample a two-month subscription.

Another newsletter I recommend is the *Growth Stock Outlook* by Charles Allmon. His record of stock picks has been excellent, and the newsletter has been among the top ten in performance over the past seven years. Again, his principles and research are consistent with what I've outlined. As I write this book, the bulk of assets Mr. Allmon manages are in cash. He's expressed publicly his feelings that the stock market is currently quite top-heavy.

Two books at the top of my list for books to read after this one would be Graham and Dodd's *Security Analysis*, the Bible of the business, offered in many MBA programs in finance. It's slow going, but if you get through it you'll have done a lot to increase your knowledge base for investing in securities.

William Nickerson's *How I Turned $1,000 Into $3,000,000 in Real Estate* has been on bookshelves for years and continues to sell well. There is a reason. In a simple, straightforward, readable style Nickerson describes how he's turned small dollars into big dollars investing in real estate. The book is an excellent extension from the real estate chapter in this book. It brings to life, through example, a lot of the principles that really can work in prudent real estate investing.

Finally, an obvious but overlooked resource is to call companies in which you're interested in investing, talk to the officers and ask them to send you their latest quarterly, annual and 10K reports. Almost always companies want to share information about themselves and will be very cooperative.

Index